Wild Canadian West

E. C. (Ted) Meyers

hancock house

ISBN 0-88839-469-1
EAN 9780888394699
Copyright © 2006 E. C. (Ted) Meyers

Cataloging in Publication Data

Meyers, Edward C.
    Wild Canadian west / E.C. (Ted) Meyers.

    ISBN 0-88839-469-1

    1. Canada, Western—History—Anecdotes. 2. Frontier and pioneer
life—Canada, Western—Anecdotes. I. Title.

FC3206.M49 2006   971.2   C00-911550-1

Printed in Indonesia — TK PRINTING

Editor: Nancy Miller
Production and cover design: Ingrid Luters

*We acknowledge the financial support of the Government of Canada through the
Book Publishing Industry Development Program (BPIDP) for our publishing activities.*

Published simultaneously in Canada and the United States by

HANCOCK HOUSE PUBLISHERS LTD.
19313 Zero Avenue, Surrey, B.C. Canada V3S 9R9
(604) 538-1114 Fax (604) 538-2262

HANCOCK HOUSE PUBLISHERS
1431 Harrison Avenue, Blaine, WA U.S.A. 98230-5005
(604) 538-1114 Fax (604) 538-2262

Website: www.hancockhouse.com
Email: sales@hancockhouse.com

Contents

This book is for Maureen

Introduction

For too many years Canadians have considered the history of the Wild West to be the exclusive domain of men and women who inhabited the southwestern states of Kansas, Arizona, Texas, New Mexico, Oklahoma and Wyoming. These places won that distinction through a combination of default and reams of print churned out by dime novelists, many of whom had never ventured west. There were occasional passing glances at Montana because of the exploits of Henry Plummer and his gang of cutthroats called, ironically, The Innocents, as well as the exploits of Virginia City's major nuisance Jack Slade. For the most part, such heavyweights as Billy the Kid, Jesse James, the Dalton boys and the Doolin gang and a few others such as Butch Cassidy or the Cimarron Kid held sway. Lawmen such as Wyatt Earp, Bat Masterson and Wild Bill Hickok still swagger their way through the history pages as the ones who stood for law and order. Few others were considered to be at their level although a great many towered above that particular trio.

The above-mentioned heroes and lawmen have no exclusive claim to the checkered history of the Old West. Canada, too, had her share of men and women, good and bad, who forged their names and deeds into the annals of what has become known as The Wild West. Not a few made their names in the American southwest. But those who tamed the rowdy towns in Canada remain, for the most part, forgotten.

Actually, truth be told, a great number of the famed gunfighters, outlaws, gamblers and lawmen of the American west were not American at all. They were Canadian. This can be startling news to people who know only the names of those who came to fame through their exploits south of the border. Conversely, a large number of those who made their marks in the annals of the Canadian Wild West were Americans who ventured north for any number of reasons. Some came in peace; others arrived one hoof-beat ahead of a pursuing U.S. marshal.

Who has not heard of Bat, Jim and Ed Masterson? To most readers of Wild West exploits they were famed Dodge City lawmen. Bat became the most famous because he knew how to tell a good story and lived long enough to write his own legend. Jim and Ed were, by far, the better lawmen of the clan, but both died young. Not one of the three was American. The Masterson brothers were all born in Quebec and lived there for years before the family moved south to Kansas after the war between the U.S. north and south (1861—65) had ended.

Butch Cassidy's gang, better known nowadays as The Wild Bunch, would not likely have attained the size it did had not George Currie, better known as "Flat Nose George," amalgamated his band of rustlers and horse thieves with Cassidy's gang. In this amalgamation Cassidy inherited Harvey Logan who went on to develop a legend of his own as the infamous "Kid Curry." The Kid chose the name Curry because he admired George, but apparently he did not know the correct spelling of his mentor's last name.

Who was "Flat Nose George?" Just a simple country boy from Prince Edward Island. George Currie decided as a teenager that Wyoming was a better bet than P.E.I. for adventure and fortune. What he found was a menial job as a store clerk in Casper. He soon traded that tedious life for one that gave him a few years of adventure and high times. The good years ended suddenly one morning when the sharp report of a sheriff's rifle shattered the still air. "Flat Nose George" Currie was twenty-seven when he died.

Ben Thompson, feared throughout four states and generally considered the deadliest gun handler who ever lived, spent some of his boyhood years in Nova Scotia after his family left his native England. He was perhaps nine when his father decided Texas held more opportunity than Canada and once again uprooted the family. Poor Ben never really knew where he had hailed from. For years he thought he had been born in Texas. Ben wasn't as swift with his mind as he was with his pistols.

"Dynamite Dick" Bartle, a deadly scourge of the California stage routes for three or four years, hailed from Montreal. He, too, died when a lawman's aim proved better than his.

"Canada" Bill Jones, generally acknowledged as the greatest card sharp of the old west, was from Ontario. So was "Cattle Kate," whose real name was Ella Watson. Ella ended her days at the end of a rope when a mob became convinced that she was a cattle rustler. She wasn't. Ella was just a harmless prostitute who operated from her shack on the outskirts of Abilene. She occasionally accepted a cow or steer in lieu of cash as she had dreams of starting a ranch and had accumulated a small herd when she was lynched.

Ella Watson wasn't the only Canadian girl to make her name south of the line. Pearl Hart, thanks to eastern writers, became one of the more famous of the lady outlaws. She was also one of the most inept.

Pearl was born in Ontario in either 1870 or 1871. When she was sixteen, she went to Globe, Arizona, and in 1889 met a miner named Joe Boot. Boot was a loser from the word Go! He was too lazy to work and Pearl's genteel Canadian upbringing caused her to shy away from getting work in a brothel, a not unusual place of employment for a young woman with no skills and a lazy "husband." Still, she and Joe had to eat; so the pair started a badger game. Pearl would stake herself out near a saloon until she saw some man, always a drunk, whom she could lure as a would-be lover to her room. There Boot would solidly caress the victim's head with a club. After the two had emptied their victim's pockets, they would drag him into a nearby alley and dump him there. When he woke up hours later, he would have no idea of what had happened to him.

Their little racket didn't last long because western characters of the type to be attracted to Pearl rarely had much ready cash so she and Joe tried stage robbery. They were no more successful in that endeavor. Over a few months they held up a number of stages but none ever yielded more than $25 until they finally hit what for them was a virtual jackpot.

One day they stopped a stagecoach not far from Globe and were delighted to lift the princely sum of $400 from the six passengers. That, however, proved to be their last robbery. Because they could not afford horses, they had to escape on foot. Following their last hold-up, the inept pair took a wrong turn in the trail, ended up in the desert and, utterly lost, wandered aimlessly for three days until they blundered back onto the main road right into the hands of an astounded sheriff and his deputies.

Both Pearl and Joe were sentenced to jail for lengthy terms. Joe Boot disappears from history at that time, but Pearl was released with a pardon several months later on condition she leave Arizona and never return. She had claimed to be pregnant insisting the father of her unborn child was either the prison chaplain or the warden. Her claim, if true, would be valid because they were the only two men who had been in contact with her.

Not wanting any publicity of that sort, the Arizona governor signed the necessary papers. There is no record of her ever having given birth but in those days unwed mothers gave up their babies for adoption so she may have been telling the truth.

Pearl joined the Buffalo Bill Wild West Show and rode with it— her part was that of a lady stage robber—for quite some time. It was during that time she became a heroine in the pulp fiction presses and her reputation as a two-gun lady and robber of stages emerged. Later, her name appears in old newspapers and court records here and there for being fined for picking pockets and streetwalking. Despite her promise never to return to Arizona, she later moved back to Globe. There she married a rancher and lived the remainder of her life in full respectability. She died at Globe about 1964. Pearl Hart would have been at least ninety-two when she died.

The list of Canadians who helped make the history of the American Wild West extends to many dozens and at times seems endless. One is tempted to speculate how they all might have fared had they stayed home.

Then there were Americans who came to Canada as if to offset the exodus of Canadians to the south. Some came north and met their fates in varying ways. Several made fortunes along the cattle trails of Alberta or in the gold fields of B.C. Many returned to their homes wealthy with the gold dust and nuggets they had extracted; but others stayed to make their marks in other ways. Several became Canadian citizens and of these some entered politics, while others opened businesses and flourished. Still others, like Bill Miner, made their names by crime. Many were jailed or hanged for their indiscretions.

Among the good people was an Irish lass, Nellie Cashman, who had gone first to Nevada, where she made a small fortune in silver mining, then to Arizona, where she made a larger fortune running a cafe in Tombstone. When she heard the news of the gold strikes in BC she headed north to try her hand at gold mining—and became a millionaire for her efforts. She also became known as "The Angel of the Cariboo" for her humanitarian work among miners less fortunate than she had been.

Another emigre was Wellington Delaney Moses, a black man, who opened a barber shop in Victoria then moved on to Barkerville where his memory remains honored as a part of gold rush history. Amor de Cosmos, whose real name was Jim Smith, came north from the California gold fields to found one of Victoria's newspapers, *The British Colonist*. He had been born in Nova Scotia but had lived for years in California, so most people thought he was American. He ran for office and eventually become one of the more colorful—and one of the least desirable—of BC's lengthy list of premiers. He died of drink and madness.

The badmen, most of whom paid for their sins, included Charlie "One Ear" Brown, who was killed by vigilantes. A Texas gambler named James Barry and Frank Spencer, a one-time Tombstone rustler and gunfighter, met their deaths at the end of ropes.

Henry Wagner, the infamous "Flying Dutchman," died in Nanaimo at the end of a rope probably wondering why he had left the comparative safety of the Wyoming hills. Wagner was probably the last of the Old West outlaws. Another Wyoming fugitive, Ernie Cashel, sought refuge in Canada only to end up on a scaffold in Calgary.

However, the Canadian Wild West had plenty of its own home-grown heroes and villains. There was really no need to import them. John Ingram was an exceptional lawman who tamed two prairie cities (first Winnipeg, then Calgary) then turned his attentions to the roaring town of Rossland, B.C. (Rossland was a wide-open town in 1895. A mining town, it had no permanent police presence. The solid citizens decided to hire a police officer and Ingram fit the bill.) His exploits behind the badge make Bat Masterson and the more famous Wyatt Earp of Tombstone appear as wimpish amateurs. One wonders what Ingram's fame might have been had he gone to Kansas or Arizona. Would he have become another Tom "Bear River" Smith, the marshal who tamed Abilene, Kansas? The two were strikingly similar in the tactics they used. And both died young. Smith was murdered; Ingram died accidentally.

Jerry Potts, arguably the most dangerous man on either side of the border, was never an outlaw but he was no saint either. Potts is credited with saving the entire first squad of the fledgling Northwest

Mounted Police from certain death in the untamed region of what is now southern Saskatchewan. He is also known to have killed at least thirty-five men before he was thirty years of age, all of them in fair fights and most of them under his blazing guns.

Then there was the Honorable Judge Matthew Baillie Begbie, the famed "hanging judge of the Cariboo" who brought justice and a respect for the law to B.C. at a time when law and order was at its weakest. He was a hanging judge who abhorred the death penalty.

Among the villains is Almighty Voice, the Terror of Batoche, who held off a posse of 100 police and civilians for nearly three days. Antoine Lucanage killed a B.C. policeman in a cowardly ambush, eluded capture for months, but eventually met a terrible death at the hands "...of person or persons unknown."

It was an unclaimed photograph that brought James Gaddy to justice. Had he not paused to indulge in the Old West fad of being photographed he would easily have made a clean escape. Gaddy and several members of Butch Cassidy's Wild Bunch have that in common—all were identified and ultimately tracked down because they could not resist the urge to pose for a photo.

Indeed, in the years from 1840–1906, the Canadian Wild West was rowdy—a time of danger, of heroes and villains, of cowards and brave people. There were gunmen, lawmen and bounty hunters. It was a time when vigilantes rode, when stage coaches were held up, when renegades, fugitives and lawmen alike could measure their immediate chances of survival by hearing the ominous *click* a pistol or rifle made when the hammer was thumbed back in the darkness of the night. He who heard the *click* had a chance to react. He who did not hear, or could not react quickly, usually died.

It was a time when fortunes were lost or won on the turn of a single card, when dreams were dashed or realized with one final swish of the gravel in a placer pan and when sudden death, accidentally or with malice intended, was met on a wilderness trail or along the banks of creeks and rivers that flowed through the valleys of western Canada. And the entire era spanned a little more than fifty years. Here are some of the stories.

— E. C. Meyers

CHAPTER 1

The Terror of Batoche

ALMIGHTY VOICE
- b. Northwest Territory, 1874
- d. near Batoche, N.W.T., May 27, 1897

The child's birth was anticipated eagerly by the father and family friends. While village women aided the mother in her delivery, the men sat outside talking and smoking dried kinnikinik leaves while they awaited the news. (Also called bearberry, the leaves of this spreading bush were much used by prairie Natives and whites as a substitute for tobacco. Unlike tobacco, kinnikinik is not addictive.) They talked of the difficult times that had befallen their people, the Swampy Cree. The theme was of increasing pessimism. Within the little circle the air hung heavy with the mild smoke produced by the leaves that had been rolled into a favored prairie version of a cigarette.

When the first lusty wails were heard from within the buffalo-hide tent the men listened attentively trying to determine if the voice was that of a boy or a girl. After a time a woman appeared from behind the tent flap to announce that the baby, a boy, had arrived. The men offered their best wishes to the expectant father then silently departed for their own homes leaving the new father to sit alone and smoke in silence. As he sat in silent meditation he reflected and watched for a sign that would guide him in choosing a name for his new son. Sometimes this took many days, but this day the decision was arrived at quickly. The wail had been the sign. The child had a lusty voice—and because he was the son and the grandson of legendary chiefs he would likely also one day be either a chief or a shaman. Either way, the sign told the father, his voice would bear the words of the Great Spirit to his people.

The child's given name, therefore, would be *Kahkeesay-mani-*

11

tou-wayo which translates from the Cree into essentially "Voice of the Great Spirit." The father felt a sense of pride. This child, he hoped, would one day become a great leader who would lead the people out of the misery they were now facing into a future of greater promise. The intensity of the voice gave some assurance of such a destiny.

Kahkeesay-manitou-wayo wailed his way into the world as the newest member of the Swampy Cree nation camped near the fledgling village of Batoche in the Northwest Territories. The year was 1874. His father, Sounding Sky, was a respected chief. His mother, Spotted Calf, was the daughter of a great chief. His paternal grandfather was One Arrow, a legendary chief. The child's lineage assured him a place in the hierarchy of the Cree nation. All he had to do was grow to adulthood with honor, pride and dignity—as his parents and grandparents had every right to expect—and he would eventually become a chief. Alas, their expectations would not come to pass. Two years later One Arrow would in great sorrow lead his people from the freedom of the prairie camps to a new and truly miserable existence within the narrow confines of a reservation that would bear his name.

Had the birth occurred a century or two earlier, One Arrow's hopes for his grandson would have been realized. But in 1874, an Indian's basic hope was that he might live as well as he could on what was available to him. The great herds of buffalo that had once roamed the prairies in vast numbers were gone. The few pitiable animals that remained were scattered in tiny groups throughout the expansive land. The days of the great hunts had ended some years before. The antelope herds, once plentiful, had been depleted and even jackrabbits, grouse and prairie chickens had begun to disappear. By 1874 the hopes of the Swampy Cree and their diverse brothers were quickly fading.

The best hope for an Indian who lived in the forested country of what is now northern Saskatchewan was perhaps to accumulate a small herd of horses for trading, develop a trapline, manage to hunt enough meat from the moose and deer that still thrived and net enough fish from the streams and rivers to feed his family through the harsh winters. For those who lived on the sweeping expanse of prairie in central Saskatchewan's Batoche area, a trapline was not a viable option. There was likewise no real possibility of him acquiring a small farm where he might raise a few cows and horses. Not only were the prairie Natives not historically an agricultural people, the federal government in Ottawa was not disposed to such schemes. Federal authorities had decided that Indians should be contained within the perimeters of reservations, accept the treaty money offered, work now and then for white farmers, guide an occasional police patrol and live in reasonable harmony with the increasing numbers of whites who even then were encroaching on the land. The world into which Kahkeesay-manitou-wayo was born did not offer him a future of much promise.

When Kahkeesay-manitou-wayo was still a very small child, he was taught rudimentary English by white men who dealt with the tribe in various capacities, some honorable and others not so principled. As these men came to know the friendly little boy they Anglicized, then shortened, his name to Almighty Voice. By the time he was nine years old it was by this name that he had became best known.

Almighty Voice got along well with the whites who spoke English, but he showed little friendship toward those who spoke French. That aversion may have come about because of his dislike of the missionaries who walked among his people insistently badgering them to forsake the traditional ways, the ways that had been the Indians' for centuries.

The French-speaking Catholic missionaries, who felt a compulsion to baptize and thereby save the immortal souls of all Indians, had arbitrarily renamed him Jean Baptiste. He hated the name and refused to answer to it. He balked at the missionaries' insistence that he learn their religion and rebuffed their demand that he learn French. As he grew older, he repudiated the name, the language and the religion they were trying to force upon him. Nonetheless, Jean Baptiste remained the name on official documents by which he was registered for treaty money and other matters.

In 1884, when he was ten, his grandfather and his father, both imagining some hope for a brighter future, threw their lot in with Louis Riel. For the duration of the ill-fated rebellion they fought under the command of Gabriel Dumont, Riel's able lieutenant. Almighty Voice spent the months of the rebellion with his mother as she tried to protect her family by hiding, running and attempting to stay clear of the many skirmishes that were fought in and around the area they saw as home. It was not a joyful period of his childhood.

When the rebellion was finally put down One Arrow was sentenced to three years in prison for his part in the uprising. There is no record showing Sounding Sky faced trial but he was fated to run afoul of the law in future episodes. Almighty Voice was shattered by the loss, however temporary, of the one adult who had some influence over him. For the next years he was haunted by the memories of the tragic battles that had raged around him. He had learned to fear and distrust whites. By the time he was fourteen he had lost all illusions.

Almighty Voice entered into his midteen years a free spirit. He now totally ignored the missionaries, shunned their teachings, refused to enter their church for the services they conducted and, when they admonished him for his conduct, told them quite bluntly that he wished to be left alone. Eventually, because the missionaries could be pragmatic when they had no choice, his wishes were honored for two very valid reasons: first, he was an acknowledged expert marksman with the Winchester rifle he always had with him and, secondly, he made it known in no uncertain terms that he would not hesitate to shoot a "blackrobe" if an opportunity presented itself. No one saw any reason to think he was bluffing, although he probably was. (The Winchester of the time was an improved .44-calibre Henry, the rifle of choice of many buffalo hunters. The new Winchester fired a bullet from a charge of 75 grains of black powder which gave it a harder wallop and a longer range than that possessed by the Henry.)

Over the next few years Almighty Voice went his own way. His disdain for mores and law was not limited to those of the white man; he showed as little respect for those of his own people. He adhered only to the ancient Cree beliefs that suited him, obeyed the ancient laws—as he interpreted them—if he felt like it, became a great worry to his parents and so alienated his friends that their numbers rapidly dwindled to a very few. What One Arrow thought of his grandson is unrecorded, but that great man must have been sorely troubled.

Almighty Voice, disregarding normal conventions, walked his own path. He cared nothing for the opinions of others. He was obviously physically attractive for he was never without female companionship. (The only picture in existence that has been associated with him—and it is not at all certain that he is indeed the subject— shows a tall, good-looking young man with shoulder-length hair and slightly effeminate features. The man in the photo stands straight and tall. He is majestic, with piercing eyes that embodies the romantic notion of the noble Indian). Almighty Voice must have been not only a handsome youth but one who was looked upon as a good provider as four women agreed to marry him—all before he was twenty. Unfortunately, he was also extremely capricious for he quickly discarded each wife, often bringing his new woman into his home even before the discarded wife had departed.

Yet, the casting off of wives was not considered a brush with the law because none of the marriages took place under Canadian legislation. His marriages were all in keeping with ancient Cree tradition. The officials were loathe to interfere in these matters being content that most Natives were adopting the Canadian laws regarding marriage and were satisfied to proceed slowly.

Almighty Voice's official sins, so far as the police were concerned, were all of a minor nature, not considered worth bothering about for they were the usual foolishness into which most teenagers become involved. He was, for the most part, a loudmouthed pain in the neck. Most of the townspeople in Batoche and Duck Lake, his usual hangouts, merely shrugged and wished he would go elsewhere.

It was not until after his death, following the familiar pattern that spawns legends, that Almighty Voice became famous. Because of his "lone wolf" behavior, he has often been romantically cast as the last "true" Indian—the noble warrior who preferred death before the dishonor of bowing to an alien law. Writers of periodicals and pulp fiction, mostly during the 1920s and 1930s, saw in him a trove of great plots. Had he lived long enough to accumulate a lengthy history, he would likely have garnered as much press as many other western outlaws becoming in the process a sort of aboriginal Robin Hood.

The usual scenario in the fictions eastern writers generated on his behalf pictures Almighty Voice as a defiant, ill-treated teenager. Finally, in desperation, he forms a small band of kindred spirits and rises up in defiance of the white man's law. Nothing could be further from the truth.

In fact, Almighty Voice was not much different from any of the other boys from the reservation. He hunted when there was something to hunt, cut hay which the reserve sold to white farmers, helped with the care and feeding of the reserve's small herd of steers and ran errands for the Batoche police detachment for food in lieu of cash. It was a frightened fifteen year old who first brushed against the "white man's" law—and it was such a minor incident it was not recorded and may have been something as simple as stealing some tobacco from a Mountie's pouch. The Mountie dealt with the errant boy by administering the punishment which was the standard of the day—a swift kick to the seat of his trousers followed by a cuff to the side of the head—then sending him home with a stern warning to stay out of trouble. Whatever the punishment was, it proved sufficient to keep the lad on the straight and narrow path for quite some time as nothing more was heard of him until he reached his twentieth birthday. Then he had another run-in with the law.

Even by the time he had reached his eighteenth birthday he was still limiting his escapades to minor things of the type most teenagers get into—trying to sneak a drink from the local saloon or firing his rifle within the confines of the town's boundaries. The police never pushed him beyond a warning. He was hardly a desperado. Perhaps the Mounties should have dealt with him a little more harshly during those early years, but they considered him as nothing more than a noisy nuisance. All in all, he would have but one serious brush with the law—and that, fatal as it was, proved his one and only moment of true infamy.

Almighty Voice's final, fatal encounter with the law began with a vagrant cow, followed weeks later by a deliberate lie told by a vindictive brother-in-law, a needless escape from the Duck Lake jail and finally the senseless killing of a member of the NWMP. It was this last act that sealed his doom.

In many ways Almighty Voice had authored his own misfortune years before by compounding his troubles on the reserve. From his fourteenth birthday onward he had never had more than two or three friends among his own people and by his twentieth birthday he had managed to alienate almost the entire population of the One Arrow Reserve.

His habit of marrying and discarding any woman he chose did nothing to endear him to the families of the women spurned. Under traditional Cree law he was within his rights, but his prospective in-laws did not approve of the indiscriminate ways he employed in discarding one woman after another as he pleased. Under traditional law a wife deemed unsuitable could be returned to her parents but such an act first had to be justified. Only then could it be finalized by the giving of gifts such as horses or buffalo robes to the woman's family. Almighty Voice, his spirit in full free flight, interpreted the canon to suit himself and refused to honor that section of the unwritten law. Besides, he owned but one horse and possessed few, if any, buffalo robes.

Of course, had the marriages been accredited under Canadian law, he would have had no right whatsoever to take more than one wife at the same time or to marry again without legally divorcing the other; but the marriages had not been made under the law. Nonetheless, Almighty Voice's marital habits kept him constantly in trouble with the Indian agent who, because of complaints laid by the missionaries, would time and time again try to convince Almighty Voice to return to his first wife and marry her under Canadian law. That would have solved some of the problem because he would have been forced to remain, at least legally, monogamous. The agent didn't care all that much but he had to appear interested because of the continuing pressure he received from the missionaries who did care.

Following each marriage, the missionaries would call upon the agent to register their displeasure. The agent would dutifully ride out to the reserve, harangue the young brave then return to town secure in the knowledge that he had done his duty. He was also well aware that Almighty Voice had absolutely no intention of paying any attention to a word he had said.

Almighty Voice's date with destiny began on the afternoon of 19 October 1895 as he was returning to the reserve from a trip into town. His mind was cluttered for the next day he would wed his fourth wife, a pretty thirteen year old named Little Face (sometimes referred to, wrongly, as Pale Face). The wedding ceremony itself was causing no problem but the feast he was expected to provide was causing him great concern. He had been unable to find payment enough to purchase meat for the entree and he was unable to find a buffalo, or even a couple of deer or antelopes that would have supplied him with sufficient meat and perhaps a bit to spare. The wedding feast was of grave concern because, despite his lack of popularity within the reserve, almost the entire population would show up for the celebrations.

It was at that moment he spotted the vagrant cow that was to begin his downfall. Without a second's thought he shot the animal, skinned and butchered it on the spot and rode his meat-laden, blood-drenched horse onto the reserve satisfied that his wedding feast problem had been solved.

Years later eastern dime novelists changed the circumstances to suggest the cow had been killed to provide food for his starving wife, broth for his ailing mother or food for the entire tribe who had fallen on hard times and were in the midst of mass starvation brought on by the greed of a crooked Indian agent. General opinion agrees he shot the cow only to provide meat for his wedding guests.

Almighty Voice killed the cow in total disregard for what should have been an obvious first thought—the animal was someone's property. But such considerations went against the grain of the philosophy he had developed: the cow was there, it was unattended, he needed meat; ergo the cow was his. One wonders what he might have done had he known the elderly, undernourished animal was to figure as the indirect cause of his ultimate fate.

Almighty Voice had been married nearly four months before the brother of discarded wife number one, already highly upset with his erstwhile brother-in-law's treatment of his sister, grew even angrier as he watched Almighty Voice cavorting with his newest bride. After brooding about the situation a day or two more he went into Batoche where he informed the Indian agent that Almighty Voice had fed his wedding guests with the meat of a rustled animal. Moreover, he upgraded the cow's status to that of a valuable bull he claimed had belonged to the reserve for breeding purposes. Later, he changed his story claiming it had been a steer that was part of the cooperative herd.

The Indian agent knew of no such bull on the reserve but could not dismiss the possibility that the animal may have been reservation property. He did, however, wonder why no one had reported its disappearance earlier. He was also curious about where Almighty Voice had obtained enough beef to feed the numbers who had attended his wedding feast, so he reported the incident to the NWMP figuring a constable might check it out when time allowed.

The constable checked into the story and actually located a farmer who may have been the lawful owner of the sacrificed animal. Ownership was never definitely established but, lacking a missing cow report from band members it seems feasible that the homesteader was indeed the rightful owner. The farmer told the Mountie that the cow, if it was his, was so old she was no longer producing milk and was not suitable for food. In fact, the farmer said, she was of such little value that when he discovered she had wandered away from the pasture he hadn't even bothered to search for her. He figured she would be eaten by coyotes before she could get very far so he didn't bother to report her missing. Both farmer and lawman marveled that she could have wandered such a distance while somehow avoiding hungry coyotes. They agreed that, despite her advanced age, she had lots of spirit for she had traversed miles of grassland and had survived for several weeks before encountering Almighty Voice and his deadly Winchester.

The police officer, though realizing that likely no crime had been committed, was bound by law to act on the brother-in-law's denouncement of Almighty Voice as a cattle thief. To that point in his life the police had never once considered him likely to "toss a long rope" (an expression denoting cattle rustling). It was decided to shelve the matter until such time as the young brave made another appearance. As a result, when Almighty Voice and a companion went to Duck Lake on 22 October to be paid treaty money, he was arrested. His companion interfered and was arrested as well.

The arrest of Almighty Voice was strictly routine; the police in Duck Lake were merely holding him until the enquiring constable, who was due back that evening, could ask him why the suggestion had been made that he was a cattle thief. The Duck Lake constable placed the two "prisoners" in a cell, told them to stay put and departed. Carelessly, he didn't lock the door. It was also unfortunate the police officer hadn't thought to explain to Almighty Voice why he was being detained.

Almighty Voice, possibly harking back to his shooting the cow, thought he had been arrested for a serious crime. Later writers stated that a brutal guard had informed him he was going to be hanged for cattle theft, but that story was just another fiction. In all likelihood Almighty Voice had no thought about being hanged but did feel he would be going to jail for whatever it was he was going to be charged with. The thought of jail did not sit well with him. His father, Standing Sky, had recently been arrested for theft and sentenced to six months in the Prince Albert jail. He knew that such a term was usually served in the NWMP stables shoveling manure. This, he decided, was too degrading to even consider so he promptly left the cell and disappeared. The following day a warrant was issued for his apprehension on charges of illegal flight. His companion was released with a warning to be less argumentative in future.

On October 29 NWMP Sergeant Colin Colebrook, on patrol

with François Dumont, a Metis guide, spotted Almighty Voice and a girl near a copse of willows. The girl was roasting a prairie chicken over a small fire. Dumont, a wily guide, sensed trouble and warned Colebrook not to approach the pair. He called out in Cree that the sergeant wished to speak to the youth. Almighty Voice replied that he did not wish to speak with the sergeant and that he would shoot if Colebrook came any closer. Dumont translated this warning and urged the officer to turn back. Colebrook refused and rode slowly forward, his rifle slung across the saddle pommel and his right hand raised, both traditional prairie symbols that the rider was approaching in peace.

Colebrook could not believe that Almighty Voice might do something dangerous. He called to him to put up his rifle as he rode slowly toward the unmounted Indian. Almighty Voice repeated his threat to shoot but Colebrook rode closer—to within a few yards. Almighty Voice raised his rifle and fired killing the officer with a single shot through the heart. Colebrook slipped from his saddle. Dumont immediately withdrew out of range.

Now realizing he would be hunted forever, Almighty Voice took Colebrook's weapons and mounted the officer's horse. He left Little Face, now crying hysterically, with the words, "Now they will never leave me alone for what I have done." And he rode hard for the woods. The guide rushed to Colebrook but the Mountie was dead. Dumont comforted the girl as best he could, told her to stay put and then rode hard for Batoche to sound the alarm.

After Colebrook's body was recovered and Little Face returned to her father, the manhunt began. It soon fizzled out for no trace could be found of the fugitive.

Almighty Voice kept on the move for weeks rarely venturing into the open and avoiding others at all times. Sometime in his travels he was joined by two younger men, a Cree named *Tupean* (a.k.a. Dubling) one of his several brothers-in-law and a fourteen-year-old boy named Standing-in-the-Sky, a cousin and member of the Salteau tribe. Both Tupean and Standing-in-the-Sky had developed a hatred for white men and their laws but their reasons have never been known. Their motives for joining Almighty Voice remain equally unclear.

For over a year the three men left no trails to follow. Many thought they had fled to Montana. They were reported as having been seen north of the Great Slave Lake and they had been "seen" in the Rocky Mountain area. A reward of $500 was posted for the apprehension of Almighty Voice. *Tupean* and Standing-in-the-Sky did not figure in the reward offer. There were no takers. In fact, the trio never ventured off the One Arrow Reserve. The Indians knew where they were most of the time and, although they may not have liked Almighty Voice, they felt it their duty to protect him for to turn him in to face the gallows was unthinkable—and of course they had to consider Little Face who was quite innocent of anything. (This loyalty did not extend to all the tribes. While it was rare for Indians to turn in a fellow tribesman for minor crimes, the killing of a police officer was a different matter.) At different times during that year, it was later determined, Almighty Voice hid in a hole under his mother's shack even as the police were talking to her.

On May 26, 1897, three men, one recognized as Almighty Voice, were seen butchering a steer, the property of ranchers David and Napoleon Venne (who eventually were paid the reward money). Napoleon rode into Batoche to report the sighting. Cpl. J. Bowridge accompanied him to the scene but the men were gone. Bowridge checked the scene carefully then he and the Vennes began a wide sweep of the immediate area. They soon found a small group of Natives nearby. Bowridge questioned them but they professed to know nothing of a rustled steer. While he was questioning the group, he spied two Indians in the distance running toward the cover of a poplar copse. Bowridge and David Venne rode to where the two had been spotted. As they approached, two shots rang out. The two men hastily retreated. Bowridge returned to Batoche to raise a posse. The Vennes returned to their ranch to guard their possessions.

The posse, a large group of police and civilians, rode out of Batoche early the following morning. As they neared the area of the last sighting by Venne and Bowridge the riders spotted Almighty Voice and another man near a large copse of poplar trees. As the posse approached, the two (the second man was identified as Tupean) ran into the bush to join a third man whom a sharp-eyed posseman identified as Standing-in-the-Sky. By noon the posse had surrounded the five-acre copse but the sharpshooting outlaws quickly inflicted three casualties among the lawmen. Sgt. C. Raven was hit in the thigh and the groin, Inspector John B. "Bronco Jack" Allen was shot off his horse with a shattered arm and Cpl. Bowridge was also wounded. Before the sun had set, the trio had wrought even further damage by killing two Mounties, Cpl. C. H. Hockin and

Constable J. R. Kerr, and a civilian posseman. Two others were wounded, one seriously.

The civilian, killed by a single shot to the chest, was Ernest Grundy, a former Mountie turned postal official who had joined the posse to assist his former comrades. "Bronco Jack" Allen, a controversial individual who was to figure prominently in later NWMP affairs, remained in charge following a quick patching.

The copse was so well covered that escape for the three fugitives was impossible, so the posse sat back to await developments. At the same time they sent word to Batoche that a heavy field piece should be brought out along with a wagon to transport the dead and wounded to Duck Lake. Throughout the night sporadic gunfire was exchanged between the two factions. (It was during this period that Tupean was killed. When his body was found, it was evident he had been dead for some time.)

During the night, before the cannon had arrived, "Bronco Jack" Allen had called on several occasions to Almighty Voice urging him and his friends to surrender. At least twice prior to nightfall he had sent two Metis guides under a white flag to the copse to ask Almighty Voice to surrender peacefully. Each time Almighty Voice replied with his booming voice:

"I am cold and hungry and thirsty. Send us some food and water. First we will eat and drink. In the morning we will have a good fight."

The sun was not yet up the following morning when a cloud of dust was seen. Two wagons, two artillery pieces in tow, lumbered into view. While the casualties were being loaded into one of the wagons, the cannons, a seven-pounder and a nine-pounder, were manhandled into positions where they could be seen plainly by the trio in the copse. Allen was determined to have his quarry surrender.

The following morning Allen relinquished command to Asst. Insp. Jack McIllree when he and a large number of reinforcements arrived from Regina. McIllree's arrival increased the posse to about 100 men.

Standing near the cannons so the outlaws could get a good look at the artillery, McIllree called to the fugitives urging their surrender. Again Almighty Voice replied with the same words he had used to reply to Allen. McIllree shrugged and ordered the cannons be primed and aimed. But before he gave the order to fire he once again sent Metis guides to the copse under the white flag. The Metis, who knew Almighty Voice was not the dastardly killer of his new-found reputation, argued long and with passion urging him to surrender. His reply ended the discussion.

"Brothers," he told them, "we have had a good fight. I am starving. Send me food and water. We will finish this fight tomorrow."

The Metis returned sadly to report to McIllree.

McIllree still hesitated to order the guns into action. He hoped the fugitives would have second thoughts. Also he was disturbed to see that a great number of Indians had assembled on a small rise some distance from the poplar grove. They had come not to rescue the trio, for that was not possible, but to begin a death watch. The plaintive voice of Spotted Calf was heard in the sorrowing timbre of the Cree death wail. She was mourning the imminent death of her son for she knew he would never surrender.

That afternoon a reluctant McIllree ordered the cannons to commence firing. An intense bombardment of the copse by both field pieces began. The outlaws returned fire and continued firing between salvos, but by late afternoon an uneasy quiet fell. During the night there were several shots fired from the trees but by 4:30 a.m. all firing from the copse had ceased. On Oct. 31 the sun rose to a deathly silence broken only by the wails of Spotted Calf from the distant hillock.

Still, the posse remained in place another cautious four hours before opening a heavy volley of rifle fire. This time there was no return fire. The encircling posse began a slow, cautious approach. At the edge of the trees the body of Tupean was found. It was obvious he had been dead for many hours, an indication he had been killed the day before or perhaps during the night while trying to escape. A short distance further Standing-in-the-Sky was discovered dead in a shallow rifle pit. When he was lifted, the lifeless body of Almighty Voice was found as well. There was little doubt that both had died of wounds received from cannon fire.

In the legend that ensued, Almighty Voice was buried where he died in the poplar grove near Batoche where he made his final stand. It seemed to the legend makers that this was a fitting end to a heroic warrior. This story, though it was for years widely believed, is untrue. Many years later, when the land had been deeded to a homesteader, the copse was cleared and the land plowed for grain planting. The plow turned up a number of items but no human remains were unearthed. The truth is that the NWMP had quietly and immediately removed the bodies of Almighty Voice and his two companions and secretly buried them in some unmarked place. The authorities were making every effort to prevent either the copse or the graves from becoming some sort of shrine.

In fact, such precautions were quite unnecessary. The Swampy Cree, especially those whose daughters and sisters Almighty Voice had defiled then discarded, were just as pleased the rascal was gone.

Indian indifference to Almighty Voice's violent demise did not discourage the legend writers of the era. The eastern press and dime novelists managed to turn the unfortunate youth into a mistreated hero in much the same way misguided zealots of the 1970s resurrected Louis Riel as a prairie freedom fighter.

Today a cairn and plaque mark the scene of Almighty Voice's final hours in Canadian western history. It was installed a few years ago by the Saskatchewan Department of Natural Resources. The plaque, a means of identifying a historical event in Canada's history, does not honor Almighty Voice. It was erected to pay respects to the posse that had run him to ground and to those he had killed during his year on the run.

CHAPTER 2

British Columbia's Hanging Judge

SIR MATTHEW BAILLIE BEGBIE
- b. England 1819
- d. Victoria, B.C, June 11, 1894

Born in England to a middle-class family, Matthew Begbie grew up as a typical English son. In childhood he was looked after by a servant until he was old enough to attend a public school, the English term for private school. Though not as prestigious as Eton, the school was creditable enough to allow him the needed scope to gain entry to a London law school. While never a truly brilliant student, Begbie attained good enough grades to graduate and he eventually found positions with a series of minor law firms. The reason for the series of different employers was that he could not hold down a job for any length of time. Corporate law, obviously, was not his forte.

Having proved that he was not a good solicitor, there remained not a shadow of a doubt that he would never enjoy success as a barrister. By age thirty-six he had been released or rejected by all the law firms with which he had ever had dealings. By the time he was thirty-seven, without a job or any prospects for one, this failed lawyer jumped at the offer of a position as judge in "the colonies," to be precise Vancouver Island on the west coast of B.C. Vancouver Island was then a colony separate from the mainland although that vast expanse of land was governed from Victoria. The position paid £800 per year, not a princely amount but better than he could really expect under his existing circumstances.

It was probably not a position he really wanted but he would at least be employed. To make matters worse his love life had been cruelly shattered when his fiancé eloped with his brother. (This incident in his life obviously devastated him as he never married. If there were women in his life, he kept them a deep secret.) Besides, the only qualifications needed for this particular colonial judgeship, in the words of Sir Edward Bulmer-Lytton, the Colonial Secretary, were an ability to read a law book and "...truss a murderer and hang him from the nearest tree." It was not necessary to know the law thoroughly because there was none, or at least precious little, in the colony at the time. Law, after all, is of little use if there are no lawmen to enforce it.

Begbie arrived in Victoria on November 16, 1858, presented his credentials to Governor James Douglas and was immediately assigned the entire area of what is now the province of British Columbia. He fell to the task with enthusiasm setting up courts here and there as the occasion demanded. He rode, canoed, walked and rode wagons from one venue to another. Some of his cases were heard in fair-sized towns, the court being a commandeered saloon, hotel lobby or town hall, while others were heard at isolated mining camps where he heard the evidence while seated in the shade of a spreading cedar tree.

He rarely stayed more than a few days as even murder cases rarely took more than one day to hear. In a single year he would cover thousands of square miles while handling a caseload that would have modern judges go mad from stress. Until 1863 Judge Begbie traveled the vast expanse of British Columbia dispensing a remarkably fair form of justice. He instilled enough fear in evildoers that he probably averted a certain amount of crime. It is safe to say he controlled the entire judicial system with an iron fist.

He became known as "The Hanging Judge," but the epithet was a misnomer; for though Begbie did sentence several men to hang, most were actually spared the rope in favor of life in prison on the personal recommendation of Begbie himself. However, these letters to the governor were such well-kept secrets they were not made public until many years after his death.

Begbie and juries did not always see eye to eye. As his feared reputation grew, juries more and more tended to find the accused "not guilty." One such jury ruled the accused was innocent because the man he killed had "died accidentally when he fell off a cliff." It mattered little to the jury that the accused had pushed him. They simply did not want to see the accused hanged. Today, judging from the evidence given in the trial records, a verdict of manslaughter would often have sufficed. In those days, however, when the charge was "capital murder," there was no gray area in which a jury—or even a judge—could move. On a charge of capital murder the jury had but two options: guilty or not guilty. The judge had but one punishment to render: death by hanging. Only the governor, and later parliament, could intervene.

When the charge was what is today called second-degree murder, a jury could also consider a verdict of "guilty of manslaughter" and the judge had a great range of punishment to consider. More and more juries returned verdicts of manslaughter rather than see a killer go to jail for the rest of his life. Often a jury would find a man not guilty rather than risk seeing him sentenced to even a term of ten years.

Begbie had his own opinions on the issue of guilt and innocence and, far from being neutral, would not hesitate to instruct a jury as to which verdict he saw fitting. When the jury went against his instructions, he could become quite irate; and on each such acquittal Begbie would give the jury members a severe lecture about civic duty as it applied to the cause of justice, no doubt making them feel as if it should be they who should be taken out to the nearest tree and strung up. However, he had no recourse but to free the prisoner, as under British law a judge could not reverse a jury's decision.

On one occasion in which the decision displeased him Begbie raged against the acquittal for a good fifteen minutes. Then he freed the accused remarking: "Prisoner in the dock, the jury has freed you. You can go—but I devoutly hope the next man you murder will be a member of this jury."

Begbie administered his version of the law during the Cariboo gold rush. Later, it was his severity which, to a great degree, may have kept the rowdy gold mine town of Barkerville from becoming another Tombstone, Arizona, (the wild western town, famous for the gunfight at the OK Corral).

Judge Begbie was reassigned to Victoria in 1875 to preside over the Supreme Court, which was then situated in Bastion Square on the waterfront. Today the courthouse, now a museum, still stands and is an imposing monument to his memory. His reputation in Victoria was such that evildoers feared to step too far out of line.

Begbie was later knighted for his services to the crown. He built a rambling house and lived the good life. His lavish spending gave birth to ongoing rumors that he had been a dishonest judge, but he ignored the rumors. Those rumors, in fact, had some basis but the original concept was incorrect. It was rumored that Begbie had invested a large amount of money in a shaft being dug by Billy Barker, the man who hit the original lode and gave the town of Barkerville its name. Such an investment, had it been made, would have represented a colossal conflict of interest. However, years later, it came to light that Begbie had invested some money in Barker's mine—but not until long after the strike had been made. This was also a conflict of interest but much less severe than had the investment been made prior to the strike. As it was, Begbie never saw a vast return on his investment because by then Barker had so many partners that dividends were spread pretty thin.

By the time Begbie retired he was already a legend and retirement gave him the leisure days to add to it. He continued his life in high society and cultivated the reputation of being a bit of an eccentric given to doing things on a whim without any pattern.

Then, after a few years had passed, his daily routine suddenly grew rigid and thereafter never varied. Every Saturday he entertained several clergy friends at a sort of ecumenical supper, which was served *exactly* at 6:00 p.m. Over supper he discussed theology with them reveling in the argument and diverse opinions and no doubt egging them on to more heated discussion. At 9:00, precisely on the stroke of the chimes, they would all be dismissed. At 9:30 a select group of sporting men (a common euphemism for professional gamblers) arrived and an all-night poker game began. The game would break up at exactly 8:00 a.m. This gave the judge ample time to prepare for the 10:30 Sunday service at the Anglican Cathedral where he sang in the choir with what a contemporary newsman remarked was "...a high, obnoxious voice."

At noon he would go to the house of retired, wealthy miner Peter O'Rielly, an old friend from the Cariboo days. (O'Reilly had also served as a gold commissioner in the Cariboo. Commissioners were responsible for the collection of taxes assessed against assayed gold.) The two would spend the afternoon reminiscing about the old days while devouring a huge rice pudding. Because they always spoke in the Chinook jargon, which the household help did not know, whatever the two talked about was, unfortunately, never disclosed or recorded.

Suddenly, in January 1894, the weekend routine ended abruptly. Begbie had learned he was dying of an incurable illness. He became a virtual recluse. Gone now were the spirited suppers with the clergy, the high-stakes poker games with the sporting men and the Sunday visits with his old friend. No one was allowed to visit, not even the faithful O'Rielly. Despite his orders, however, he had many friends with him when he died on June 11 simply because he was much too weak to force them to leave. In all likelihood he was not aware of their presence.

Sir Matthew Begbie left an estate so small that there was doubt it would cover his debts. It did, however, put to rest any thoughts of his dishonesty. Nonetheless, by the time his debts were paid there was enough money left to honor his two bequests. A small amount of cash was made available to a group of homeless men and women he had befriended; and to each of his clergy friends he left $100 plus either a case of claret or one of sauterne, whichever they so desired. He made no provision to mix and match stating that the case each chose was what they got.

The funeral was well attended, including even some of the men he had tried over the years. Following the service a long cortege wound its way along familiar streets to the Ross Bay cemetery. There he was laid to rest under a simple wooden cross on which his friends inscribed his final words: "Lord, be merciful to me, a sinner."

Besides The Hanging Judge, Begbie had also been known as The Tyrant Judge and The Terror of the Cariboo depending on the respective outlooks of those who knew him or had dealings with him. Regardless of what he was called he had tamed and ensured that a rowdy territory would remain peaceable to as great a degree as was possible under the wilderness conditions of the times. He had brought a brand of tough, frontier justice to the goldfields, the ranch country, the fishing villages and the lumber towns. Later he tackled Vancouver Island and produced similar results there.

The City of Victoria later named a street in his honor. Begbie Street is a tree-lined avenue, generally peaceful and quiet, the kind of place Judge Begbie had always wanted his jurisdiction to become.

CHAPTER 3

The Face In the Nugget

JAMES BARRY
- ◆ b. Texas, circa 1835
- ◆ d. Richfield, B.C., August 8, 1866

James Barry arrived in Canada in either 1864 or 1865. He has been described as a professional gambler who was no stranger to frontier mining towns in the United States. However, his life to that point is not well known for he was a secretive fellow who remained for the most part uncommunicative, at least as much as was possible, to those he met along the way. Those who had occasion to travel with him, mostly in coaches and wagons although he occasionally joined a group of riders, said later they were well aware he carried a couple of .44-caliber pistols and none had reason to doubt his ability or willingness to use them. There were few who remained his companion longer than was necessary, for there were things about his mannerisms that warned people away. He never said from whence he had come but a soft, accentuated drawl indicated a southern state, more than likely eastern Texas. There was also the suspicion that he had seen the inside of the occasional American jail. This hunch was to be later reinforced at his trial in 1866 when he stood before Judge Matthew Begbie to answer a charge of capital murder.

When he eventually made his way north, probably from the gold fields of California, it was to Victoria he gravitated because of the large, mostly transient, colony of fellow-Americans already there. His reason for coming to Canada has never been certain but he was likely lured north by the promise of riches to be found in the B.C. gold fields. Not that he planned to dig or pan for the yellow metal—Barry shunned hard work of any sort. His intention was to relieve others of the gold they had wrenched from the earth. The method he envisioned was through the fall of cards on a green baize-covered gaming table or through theft. Barry employed either method. During Barry's sojourn in Victoria he gambled here and there in whichever saloon had an opening for a house gambler. A house gambler was one who was paid a set fee to operate a faro board for the saloon owner or the board owner. The hourly fee for such service was usually up to eight dollars on shifts of eight to twelve hours. A good faro dealer could make three or four hundred dollars a week without risking a penny of his own money. Of course, there was also the chance to skim a few dollars off the take if the dealer was experienced in such things as Barry undoubtedly was.

The big money, though, was in playing poker at a table of one's own. Most professional gamblers, those who were very gifted at poker in all its variations, preferred the latter plan. These men (there were also several women gamblers in the Old West) paid the saloon management rent for a table. The payment was either cash up front, a percentage of the winnings or a set amount from the ante from each game played. In very busy saloons all three methods could combine depending on how badly a gambler wanted a table of his own. Barry, as did many others, may have dealt faro for an hourly wage in one saloon then played poker at his leased table in another. There is no record of his prowess as a card player, but his talent appears to have been limited for he was very often broke, not an enviable situation for a professional gambler.

Whatever Barry's status may have been, he did not stay long in Victoria. His departure was either because the gambling opportunities proved too lean for his scope or he went broke in a run of bad luck. Gamblers, even the best professionals, then as now, remain subject to the whims of fickle fate. He left for the mainland to spend the autumn and winter of 1865 in and around New Westminster dealing faro and playing poker in two or three of that city's numerous saloons.

Those who gamed at his table saw him as an unfriendly sort (not unusual in a gambler), but there is no hint that he was dealing a dishonest game—at least no one ever caught him cheating. If he was perhaps dealing from elsewhere in the deck other than the top, he did so discreetly. It seems likely he also entered into various criminal activities because it is known he spent a couple of months on the local prison's chain gang paying a debt to society.

When the spring thaw melted the ice and snow in the interior enough to allow resumption of the search for gold many hundreds of hopeful men—and not a few women—headed north once again. In March, 1866, Barry also turned his back on New Westminster, bought a stage ticket and set out for Barkerville, a roaring camp town that was the newest gold capital of the great west. (Barkerville, during the heyday of its gold strike, became the largest town in the Canadian west. Its population was, for a few years, second only to San Francisco, California.) He told his fellow passengers that he was heading for Quesnelmouth, but that his intention was to go on to Barkerville to establish a gaming table in one of the new town's ubiquitous saloons. (What is left of Quesnelmouth is a collection of weathered shacks and other buildings. There is a move afoot to restore it as a tourist attraction. The bustling town of Quesnel took over in size and importance many years ago.) However, he confided to one passenger, a man named Fraser, that he was dead broke. Fraser loaned him five dollars.

Fraser later began to feel a mite uneasy with Barry because he got the impression that one of the guns Barry was carrying had been stolen from one of Fraser's friends; and Barry seemed to know more than an average man should have known about a series of unsolved robberies that had taken place in New Westminster during the winter.

When the stage arrived at Quesnelmouth the apprehensive Fraser took leave of Barry and teamed up with a couple of other, presumably less intimidating, men. Fraser was to supply the B.C. police with valuable information about his erstwhile traveling companion within a few months. In the meantime he cleared his mind of his three-day association with Barry. It is not known if Barry ever repaid the five dollars.

Quesnelmouth at the time was the stage terminus as the trail to Barkerville, narrow and rough, was not suitable for cumbersome five- and six-horse stage coaches. Those who wished to continue to Barkerville walked the remaining forty miles unless they were lucky enough to catch a ride with a wagon heading that way. Some, very few, had access to a horse. (To western fans brought up on a diet of Hollywood movies it comes as a bit of a surprise that few people actually owned a horse. The cost of upkeep was prohibitive. Cowboys, for instance, rode horses owned by the ranchers for whom they worked. Most westerners rented horses if they had need to ride somewhere. Otherwise, they traveled by stage or rail.)

Quesnelmouth, in March, 1865, teemed with men heading for the Barkerville area with high hopes; and by September with as many who were returning, some with gold in their pokes but most with only broken dreams. It was while he was in Quesnelmouth that Barry met two men who were also heading to Barkerville. In making their acquaintance he sealed the fate of one of the men and his own as well.

One of the men was Charles Morgan Blessing, the thirty-year-old scion of a wealthy American industrial family. Not wishing to merely sit back to enjoy the family fortune while waiting to take over management of the family business, he had journeyed north in the hopes of establishing his own personal fortune by striking it rich in the newly discovered gold creeks. Blessing, however, was not intending to operate on a shoestring. He had access to money from home should he hit a major lode that would require drill and excavating equipment, sluices, etc. For immediate expenses he carried an amount of cash estimated to have been more than sixty dollars, about five hundred dollars by today's standards. He was what might be called "flush" when he met up with Barry.

The other person was a black man named Wellington Delaney Moses who owned the best barber shop in Barkerville. Moses was from the Grand Cayman Islands, was a British subject and had a better than average education. What is also known about the man is that he was a very good barber, an astute judge of people and an excellent businessman. He had operated a successful barber shop in Victoria since 1858 and had garnered many loyal customers and good friends along the way. His shop in Barkerville proved to be no less successful.

He was also a bit of a con man for he sold bottles of a mysterious lotion made from a "secret" recipe, which he guaranteed would restore hair during the preliminary onset of baldness. On his sign was the hopeful message:

If your HAIR is falling, call and have it RESTORED
before you are baldheaded

Perhaps his cure had some effect because the ads he ran in the Barkerville newspaper always contained testimonials from many people who swore by the remedy.

One of the refinements of his Victoria shop had been a bathtub which his customers could use at a reasonable cost. The bathtub, secluded in a corner behind privacy drapes, had abundant hot water and came supplied with towels and soap. It brought only a marginal profit to Moses because the water, which was delivered to his shop by wagon at a cost of $1 for forty buckets, added to the overhead. There was also the cost of heating the water. Nonetheless, Moses had kept his sideline as a service to his grateful customers. He had not carried over this service to Barkerville, however.

Moses earned a high measure of respect in Victoria's overall population and was gaining notice from the small but increasing black community that was springing up in Victoria. Had he stayed, and had he harbored political ambitions, he may well have seen himself elected to some political post, albeit minor given the times. His restless nature, and an eye for the women, however, dictated that he move on. Also, his wife was so unhappy with his roving eye she had attempted to drown herself but had been rescued whereupon she returned to England leaving Moses to philander at will. When the goldfields at Barkerville opened Moses saw new opportunity and decided he should get in on the action. He sold his shop and set out for the booming goldfields where he established the area's first barber shop. He later expanded his business to include a mens' clothing store.

That Moses was financially successful is obvious for he was able to close his shop each autumn when the snow began to fall and return to Victoria where he spent each winter. Only wealthy and moderately wealthy men could take advantage of that particular luxury.

Moses and Blessing met somewhere along the road between New Westminster and Yale. Blessing was making his way to stake a claim on William's Creek, near Barkerville, and Moses was returning to reopen his shop for the summer. The two had taken an instant liking to each other. In the vernacular of the times they became "chummies" and decided to travel together. Moses had also decided Blessing, being green to the wild west, needed a guardian because of his careless habit of exposing too much of his bankroll whenever he had to pay for something. Moses, wise in the ways of the west, decided to keep a close eye on the gullible easterner.

Somewhere along the way Moses happened to remark that the stick-pin in Blessing's string tie was of an unusual shape. Blessing, who was proud of the pin, removed it and showed Moses how it resembled a man's head and face when viewed from a certain angle. It was then that Moses realized the pin was a gold nugget. That pin was destined to play an important role in the months to come.

Barry meanwhile had arrived in Quesnelmouth and met Blessing and Moses by chance at a hotel the two had decided to stay in overnight. They were making arrangements for their beds when Barry, who was sitting alone in the lobby, caught sight of Blessing's money pouch. He sidled over, mentioned his pleasure at meeting a fellow countryman, made some small talk then asked if the two would join him in the saloon for a mug of beer, or "bitter" as it was more commonly called. How pleased he was at meeting Moses is suspect because of the racial prejudice of the day but he knew the two were together so he was forced to bluff it.

Moses, on the other hand, did not like Berry one bit but for a different reason. He had spotted the man as a gambler, took note of the pistol concealed under his waistcoat and surmised that Barry had caught a glimpse of the roll of bills on Blessing's person. Moses deduced the man intended to lure Blessing into a card game. He tried to warn the garrulous young man that the gambler was potential trouble but Blessing shrugged off the warnings. He replied that he and his companion would be pleased to partake of a pint of bitter with Barry. Over the beer Blessing and Barry decided the three should journey together the remaining forty miles to Barkerville. Moses agreed, but only to keep an eye on Barry.

As the evening unfolded Blessing and Barry decided to stay a couple of extra days in Quesnel. Moses, because he had to arrive in Barkerville early enough to open his shop, was not anxious to stay. He tried to talk Blessing into going with him. But Blessing felt Moses had incorrectly judged Barry as a threat. He dismissed Moses' fears. Thus rebuffed, Moses went on ahead perhaps convincing himself that his suspicions about Barry were indeed unfounded. He was later to regret his decision. The following morning he bid adieu to Blessing and joined a group of men on the trail to Barkerville.

"If something should happen to me," Blessing had told his chummie, "remember my name is Charles Morgan Blessing. I would like you to notify my family."

They were the last words Moses would hear from his friend.

Barry had indeed discovered that Blessing was carrying a large amount of cash and had decided to take it. He was quickly disappointed to find that Blessing was not a card player nor did he harbor any intention of becoming one. This was a setback as Barry could hardly just steal the money outright. He was well aware that B.C. lawmen had a well-earned reputation for solving crimes and were sure to catch him quickly. Also, Moses was a problem. Barry may have considered robbing Blessing somewhere on the trail then framing Moses for the crime, but if he had such a thought he dismissed it as too risky. He knew such a tactic might have a chance of success in Texas but it would not likely convince the lawmen in B.C. for Moses was too well known. He would be forced to make another plan, one with a chance of being successful. When Blessing agreed to stay another day or two he was delighted. When Moses announced he would be leaving the following morning, Barry was positively elated.

Barry and Blessing remained in Quesnel for two more days. They seemed to be getting along well but it was noted, and duly mentioned later, that Blessing was doing all the buying as Barry seemingly had very little money. On May 31, in the early morning, the two men set out alone on the road to Barkerville. Around noon, having walked a little more than half the distance, they stopped, built a small fire a few yards off the trail and cooked a bit of lunch.

Barry had chosen the spot because it was on a straight stretch of the road, a place where he could see both directions for a long distance. Surprisingly there had been few travelers on the trail and none had asked to join the pair. The two watched a cowhand with a small herd of skittish cattle driving the animals along the dusty trail. They watched as he herded the animals past their camp. The drover made no signs of seeing them, however, and neither Blessing nor Barry hailed him.

When the drover and his herd passed out of sight and beyond sound range Barry extinguished the fire as if to resume the journey. As Blessing, his back to Barry, placed the utensils into their packs Barry looked both ways to check the road then drew one of his pistols and shot Blessing in the back of the head. Blessing was dead within a fraction of a second.

Barry quickly removed the dead man's money from his pouch then covered the body with leaves and debris. But he, perhaps because of haste, made two mistakes that would prove to be the gravest errors of his entire life. The first error was his failure to remove all identification from his victim's pockets. His second error was made when he removed the unusual stick-pin that Blessing wore in his tie. It was the pin that eventually placed the noose around Barry's neck.

Barry concealed the body (poorly as it turned out), obliterated all signs of the fire, removed anything that indicated the site had been used as a resting place then continued on to Barkerville. There he set up his gambling table in one of the town's saloons. As the weeks passed, he enjoyed success at cards. Blessing's money had provided him with a fine stake.

Moses meanwhile had reestablished his thriving business and was doing his usual brisk trade. He was curious that his friend had never arrived but as the days slipped by decided that Blessing may have proceeded directly to William's Creek and bypassed Barkerville. He probably would have forgotten completely had it not been for three circumstances. One morning in August he had a chance meeting with Barry and in a further coincidence a few days later he met Fraser, Barry's erstwhile traveling companion.

That he had not seen Barry in town during the three months just past was not unusual. The roaring town had so greatly increased in population that men came and went in great numbers sometimes not seeing even their own partners for days or weeks at a time. As well Barry was a habitué of the saloon scene and Moses was not. While Barry plied his trade at night, Moses ran a day business. It was sheer coincidence that put the two together that morning.

Barry, whose attitude toward black men was less than friendly, would not have even spoken to Moses had Moses not spoken to him. He asked what had become of Blessing. Barry, knowing he might have to answer such a question eventually, had concocted a story.

"Blessing?" he said, casually. "Oh, he had second thoughts about his mining venture. We were all ready to leave when right out of the blue he told me his feet were too sore to walk any more. I guess the northern wilderness was not to his liking. Said he was goin' back to the States. Caught the next stage south, he did."

Barry paused to see what reaction the statement might invoke. Seeing nothing to suggest suspicion on Moses' part he turned and continued on his way.

Moses might have bought the story had it not been for the second occurrence. After all, Blessing would not have been the first to turn his back on the rigors of northern B.C. His concern, however, increased sharply when he spotted his friend's unusual tie-pin adorning Barry's cravat. He did not say anything about it to Barry. Moses said nothing to anyone at the time, but it bothered him nonetheless. Then, a few days later the third event manifested itself. Fraser, Barry's uneasy companion on the stage from New Westminster to Quesnel, decided to get his hair cut. During the course of conversation the subject switched to the excess of gamblers and lowlifes in town. Fraser complained how the saloons were managing to extract the miners' gold faster than it could be dug or panned. Fraser was also concerned that the saloon girls and the "hurdies" had become a few too many. (Hurdies was short for hurdy-gurdy girls. These were buxom women, mostly from Germany and Holland, dressed in colorful outfits common to the mountain regions of Europe. Hurdies worked in saloons and dance halls with the singular purpose of exploiting miners who had dollars and/or gold. They did this by dancing with the lonely men for 10¢ to 25¢ a dance.) Moses replied he knew only one gambler by name and mentioned Barry. Fraser told Moses that he also knew the man and didn't like him one bit. Fraser considered him too slick to be running a fair game but had to admit he had no proof that this was the case.

Fraser's discourse on Barry renewed Moses' curiosity about the stick-pin. After Fraser departed Moses closed his shop and went to the local police office where he voiced his misgivings to Chief Constable William F. Fitzgerald, the officer in charge.

At first Fitzgerald was doubtful of Moses' concerns but he became very interested when Moses mentioned the stick-pin and the story behind it. The officer agreed that things may very well be wrong. He told Moses to say nothing to anyone and to avoid Barry at all costs if he could while Fitzgerald made some discreet enquiries.

The police officer, that very afternoon, was about to begin an investigation when he was informed a body had been discovered by a miner hunting his dinner. Fitzgerald and Constable John Sullivan rode out to the site to investigate the find. They had no trouble deciding they had a murder on their hands. Then they found the identification that Barry had so carelessly overlooked. The officers hastened back to Barkerville intent on questioning Barry about the murder of Charles M. Blessing.

Despite their attempts to keep the discovery low-key, word that the police had identified a body found near the trail made its way back to Barkerville. The news traveled quickly and Barry, hearing the news and knowing he would be a suspect, hastily packed his gear and hurried through back trails to Quesnelmouth intent on catching a stage that would take him south to the safety of the border.

Sullivan and Fitzgerald were late getting back to town and searched for Barry only to discover that he had not been seen anywhere for several hours. Finally someone recalled he had left town hurriedly. Fitzgerald told Sullivan to get a horse saddled and head for Quesnelmouth. Perhaps Barry could be apprehended before he got on the stage.

Sullivan, an experienced man-hunter, suggested instead that he bypass Quesnelmouth. He felt Barry had too big a jump on pursuit and even a lumbering stage would be impossible to overtake. Sullivan felt he should take a trail he knew that cut southwest to Soda Creek and took many miles off the distance. Its only drawback was that it was a rough trail that took hours even for a good horse and rider to navigate. It might, however, get him into Soda Creek ahead of the stage. Fitzgerald told him to do as he pleased so long as he returned with Barry.

The constable saddled his favorite horse, a small, tough western mustang long on wind and a match for any mountain trail, stuffed his saddlebags with enough supplies for a two-day ride and within the hour was on the trail heading for Soda Creek, 120 miles distant.

Unfortunately, he was unable to cover those 120 miles of rough trail as quickly as he had hoped. Upon arrival at Soda Creek he was informed by the manager of the stage way-station that a man matching Barry's description had arrived two days before, not by stage but by a riverboat that made regular runs between Quesnelmouth and Soda Creek. Barry, always wily, had shunned the stage knowing it would be watched. The fugitive had then booked passage on the next stage to Yale; and it had left the day before.

Sullivan was crestfallen. He could never overtake the stage despite the time it would take for that lumbering conveyance to reach Yale. His mustang, sweat-streaked and blowing hard, could not be pushed further. Even with a fresh mount and riding well into the night he would still be fifty miles behind when the stage pulled into Yale. By the time he arrived in Yale, Barry would have been able to walk to the border and safety.

The discouraged constable was staring upward as if entreating some good spirit to offer him sound advice when his gaze fell upon a single wire that glistened in the sunlight. The good spirit had heard him. It had directed his eye directly to the one thing that would solve his problem. The telegraph wire, recently installed from Yale to Quesnelmouth had not bypassed Soda Creek. Constable Sullivan turned on his heel and reentered the way station.

"Is that wire outside the new electric telegraph?" he asked.

"Yessiree. And brand new she be, too," the station keeper replied. "Puts us in touch with all the stations from Yale to Quesnelmouth. Solves a lotta problems, she does."

"If I get you to send a message to Yale do you think the station manager would take it over to the B.C. police office there?"

"Sure he would. All you'd hafta do is let him know it's real important. Is it about the bozo you be chasing?"

"Yes, it is," Sullivan said. "I'll write the wire and you send it right away. You can do that?"

"Yessir," the manager replied. "Write your message. I'll have the operator send it right off. It'll be there in a couple of minutes."

Sullivan hurriedly composed his message, handed it to the station manager then waited as the operator tapped the dots and dashes that were about to seal James Barry's fate.

"By the way," the operator volunteered, "I added that the police send a reply here so you'll know how it's all turning out. Was that alright?"

"Sure was. Thanks. I have to look after my horse. Where's the stable?"

The manager gave the directions, then invited the officer to have supper with him and his wife, an invitation that was gratefully accepted. Then Sullivan went to attend to his near-blown horse.

Barry was feeling safe now. The stage had rumbled into Yale right on schedule. The five-horse team was slowed to a trot as the driver skillfully maneuvered the coach along the narrow main street. (Stages in B.C. at the time were pulled by teams of either five horses or six horses. The six-horse teams were harnessed in pairs and the five-horse teams ran three horses abreast up front with two behind. The five-horse teams had better pulling power because of the extra horse on the drive line.) Barry, peering from the small square window, was pleased to note no sign of activity that might indicate his flight was known. He had covered 400 miles from Barkerville in less than four days and was now only forty miles from the border. He would walk the distance, he decided. Better avoid the open road to move along the trails where he wouldn't cause any notice. Once south of the line he would be safe. The team, panting and snorting, drew up in front of the stage depot.

"Yale," called the driver. "All passengers get out and stretch. Those going on to New Westminster will be changing coaches here so take your baggage with you."

James Barry grabbed his carpetbag, stepped off the stage, staggering a little as his legs, accustomed to the swaying of the stage, got used to the steadiness of the ground below. To his great dismay he found himself staring directly into the chest of a police officer who had been waiting for him to step off the stage. James Barry had become the first fugitive in B.C. to be trapped by a telegraph wire.

"James Barry," the police officer intoned, "you are being detained as a material witness to a murder committed near Barkerville on or about May 31 of this year."

Barry instinctively denied knowing anything about a murder. He wasn't from Barkerville. He didn't know a James Barry. The police officer merely shrugged. Then Barry again denied being James Barry and gave a false name. The lawman replied that he intended to hold him in custody until the name could be checked. Barry then insisted that he had rights because he was an American citizen. The officer assured him that indeed he had rights which would all be safeguarded, but at the moment, American or not, he was subject to Canadian law. By this time the pair had reached the town's jail and on that note the officer guided the still protesting Barry into a cell and slammed the door.

Again the telegraph wire hummed with activity. This time it would inform Constable John Sullivan that Barry had been apprehended and was in secure custody. The next morning he saddled his horse, rode to Yale, took charge of his prisoner and formally charged him with murder. The following day Barry and Sullivan returned by stage to Quesnel where a wagon awaited for the journey to Barkerville. There, Barry would be held in custody to await his trial at Richfield, a small settlement near Barkerville. (Barkerville was actually three settlements in one. Two smaller towns, Richfield and Camerontown, were but a stone's throw from the larger settlement.)

☞   ☞   ☞

James Barry's trial began early on the second Thursday in July, 1867, before the Honorable Matthew Baillie Begbie, the so-called "hanging judge" and a jury. From a large group of miners and other residents, a panel of "...twelve men, all good and true..." were selected to sit as jurors. Begbie asked the prosecution, represented by Mr. H. P. Walker and the defense lawyer, Mr. A. R. Robertson if they were prepared to proceed. Both replied in the affirmative.

All that day a parade of witnesses came forward to tell what they knew of the case. The first to testify was Chief Constable Fitzgerald who told how he had been approached by Wellington Moses, a resident, who had voiced concerns about one Charles Blessing who was missing. He told of his investigation, where and how the body of Charles Blessing had been found, its condition and of the massive bullet wound to the back of the head that had caused instant death. Fitzgerald also testified how he had learned of one of the prime exhibits in the case, the gold nugget with the strange shape that held the likeness of a human face.

He told of confronting Barry with the nugget asking him how come it had been in his possession. Barry, he testified, had first told him he had never seen the pin before. Fitzgerald had then informed his prisoner that the stick-pin had been found in the possession of a saloon girl who readily admitted to having received it as a gift from Barry. Barry then had told Fitzgerald he had bought the nugget from an American he had known in Victoria.

Constable John Sullivan took the stand next. He told of his part in the initial investigation and his ride to Yale in pursuit of the accused. He then repeated much of what Barry had told him on the return journey including a story of how Barry had "...seen several Chinamen on the trail..." and that Barry thought maybe they "...had done in the poor fellow." The saloon girl was not called but her written statement that the oddly shaped nugget had been given to her as a gift by James Barry was read into the record.

At that point the nugget/stick-pin was introduced as an exhibit. It was passed to Judge Begbie who looked closely at it, easily saw the face and was so impressed by the unusual quality of the piece that he sketched a quick drawing in his bench book. (The bench book including the sketch is on file in the B.C. Archives, Victoria.) The nugget then passed among the jury members. Each inspected it closely.

Wellington D. Moses was the first civilian witness called to the stand. His testimony proved the most damning of all. He described in detail the nugget, his chance meeting with Barry the previous August and the explanation Barry had given in reply to his enquiries about Blessing. Moses, well known and as highly respected in Barkerville as he had been in Victoria, was listened to with rapt interest.

Mr. H. P. Stark, a miner, was then called. He testified that he had seen Blessing and Barry together at a hostelry known as 13 Mile House on May 31. His testimony shattered Barry's story that he had left Blessing in Quesnel.

The final witness was Patrick Gannon, the drover with the skittish herd. He testified he was driving a small herd of cattle toward Barkerville and had seen Barry and Blessing sitting near a campfire having lunch a few yards from the place the body had been found. He said that he had not talked to, or even acknowledged their presence, because he was having trouble keeping his cattle under control and had passed by quickly.

Judge Begbie then called the defense to open its case. Mr. Robertson, who had already cross-examined the prosecution witnesses, called two or three witnesses who spoke of their dealings with the accused. None could give much testimony and none could vouch for Barry's alibi. Robertson, an able lawyer, made as good a defense as possible considering he had little to work with.

Judge Begbie then gave his instructions to the jury. He summed up the case, pointed out parts of the testimony that could not be considered in the deliberations and bade the twelve jurors to give proper and due regard to an effort to arrive at a fair and just verdict. He reminded them that under British law no one can be found guilty if there is a shred of doubt and that the verdict must be unanimous. He reminded the jurors, some of whom were American citizens and therefore more familiar with American law, that they must not confuse the differences with British law. (American law stated the accused could appeal but not the state. If acquitted, the accused could not be charged again—double jeopardy. American juries could bring in a lesser verdict if they felt like it. British law was rigid on "capital murder." American judges could override a jury's verdict, but a British judge could not.)

It was late in the afternoon when the grim-faced miners of the jury filed into a small back room to consider the evidence and arrive at a verdict. The verdict: "Guilty as charged."

Judge Begbie, who despite his reputation as a "hanging judge" was not an adamant champion of the death penalty, thanked the jurors then spoke directly to Barry. He asked him if he wished to speak prior to the sentence being passed. Barry repeated that he was not guilty but otherwise had nothing to say. Begbie then quietly intoned the mandatory sentence—death by hanging. He set the date of execution for August 8 and adjourned the court.

In those days an appeal was automatically entered to the governor in Victoria. The appeal was heard at the end of July by James Douglas, the governor at the time. Douglas denied the appeal. The verdict and sentence would stand.

As the sun rose across the mountains on August 8, 1867, its warming rays fell across a crudely built scaffold that had been erected the previous evening. Because executions in that era were public, a medium-sized crowd had already gathered.

At eight o'clock, two men were removed from their cells but all eyes were on James Barry. (The other hanged man was Nikel Palsk, a Native who had murdered a miner. His trial had preceded that of Barry. Nothing is known of Nikel Palsk.) The two were led from jail accompanied by a Catholic missionary, Father McGuicken, and the chief constable. The four crossed the enclosure to the gallows where the prisoners were assisted up the steps to the platform. Neither spoke last words. Hoods were placed over their heads. Each man had a noose slipped around his neck, the knot snugged against base of his right ear, forcing his head slightly to the left. The priest began a short prayer, was halfway through the text when, at a nod from the chief constable, a wedge was knocked away from a restraining plank. The trap fell out from under the condemned mens' feet. At 8:30 a doctor pronounced Barry dead whereupon the body was lowered to the ground. The second man was pronounced dead a few minutes later. The crowd quickly dispersed. By nine o'clock the gallows had been taken apart.

Wellington Delaney Moses remained in Barkerville. Following the great fire in 1868 that destroyed the town, Moses rebuilt not only his barbershop but increased his interests to include a mens' wear store. He remained in Barkerville even after most of the gold had petered out and the town had decreased both in size and commerce. During the summer of 1890 he took ill and died. Because of the standards of the times, he was buried in the graveyard designated for Orientals and other nonwhites. That cemetery is just outside Barkerville. When the old ghost town was reconstructed as an historic attraction some years ago, his barber shop was one of many buildings restored to their original condition and appearance. The sign depicting the wonders of his cure for baldness hangs proudly above the entrance.

Constable John Sullivan remained in the B.C. police for many years as did Chief Constable W. H. Fitzgerald.

Following the discovery of Blessing's body, a committee of Barkerville citizens took up a collection and raised in excess of one hundred dollars. With the money they paid for a funeral service and a coffin for Charles Blessing. He was buried very near the spot he had been gunned down by James Barry. The money proved enough to also pay for a fine wooden headboard plus a fence of white pickets to surround the gravesite. It, too, has been refurbished and can still be seen to this day. The site is 42.5 kilometers from Quesnel.

There were no collections taken for James Barry; neither were tears shed. He was interred without ceremony somewhere in the Barkerville graveyard in a grave unmarked and with no known record denoting its location. The man who came to B.C. under unknown circumstances was fated to remain there without leaving any evidence of where he would slumber in his final repose.

CHAPTER 4

The Mysterious Riders

◆ BOUNTY HUNTERS IN WESTERN CANADA (1867–1900)

Sitting motionless in the saddle, he peered down from his position atop a hillock into the clearing a hundred yards below. The night was as dark as the inside of an abandoned mine, the only light being that from the moon when it occasionally emerged from behind a cloud. The rider, a hunter of men, eyes fixed on the tiny flicker of a campfire below, dismounted and tethered his horse to a bush. Again he looked down at the clearing. His first view had not deceived his eyes for there was but one man and one horse. The man was seated facing the fire. The butt of a pistol protruded from the holster attached to the man's belt. He saw also that the man had propped a rifle against a tree scant inches away from his grasp. The horse, unbridled and bare of saddle, stood quietly near the edge of the little clearing munching without concern on a carpet of clover. That the horse was devoid of harness was significant. Obviously the man felt safe. His having risked a fire, however small, further attested to this. The hunter unsheathed his rifle, a .44 Winchester, and quickly inspected the lever mechanism. He levered a shell into the breech, set the hammer at half-cock as a safety measure then, quietly and carefully, picked his way down the narrow pathway to the vale bottom. He moved stealthily, slowly, silently so as not to disturb rocks and pebbles underfoot. A dislodged stone could make enough noise to spook the horse who would whinny or snort thus alerting the man who sat hunched near the fire. Even the cry of a nighthawk could become the signal that would send the man scurrying for cover his rifle at the ready.

As the hunter crept cautiously toward his prey, he caught glimpses of the man's face as the small fire cast its light upon him. There was no mistake. The man huddled before the fire, sipping from a tin cup brimming with steaming coffee, was the face on the wanted poster tucked inside the hunter's jacket. There was no doubt; this was the outlaw the hunter had tracked through the dense forests of Montana and Idaho to this lonely valley in eastern British Columbia. It had been a long trail and here the trail would end.

The hunter eased himself to a kneeling position, silently thumbed the rifle's hammer back to full cock, raised the weapon to his right shoulder, sighted through the open V rear sight until the cylindrical bead, the front sight at the end of the barrel, jutted ever so slightly above the bottom of the V. He slowly raised the rifle upward until the outlaw's head was aligned with the sights. He squeezed the trigger and the Winchester barked a one-note song of death.

The man at the fire fell sideways, shuddered once and died. Perhaps the last sound he heard was the rifle's report echoing through the confining hills. Then his world fell dark, forever silent. The horse, frightened, reared and strained against the rope that held him tethered.

The hunter approached the fallen man with caution, rifle at the ready. He toed his right boot under the fallen man's shoulder, eased the body onto its back for a good look at the face. He cared not that he had killed the man. The poster made the rules:

Wanted! Dead or Alive

To the hunter, the man lying in death on the ground at his feet was nothing more than a $500 reward.

The hunter turned and hurried back along the path to retrieve his horse. He would spend the night here, he decided, then, come sunup, would tie the body across the saddle of the outlaw's horse, cross the border back into Washington Territory and deliver him to the sheriff's office at Bonner's Ferry. There he would fill out the forms and claim the reward. He would be asked no questions; the poster made that clear.

Meanwhile, he would make some supper from the outlaw's supplies. No use wasting anything—and the coffee smelled good, too. He sat down beside the fire and refilled the dead outlaw's tin mug from the pot that still simmered at the edge of the fire.

Does that scene appear familiar? It should. It has been played and replayed many times in hundreds of Hollywood B movies over the years. But could it be true? Was it not the product of a screen-writer's prolific pen? The answer is: both are correct. The only real difference is that the Hollywood bounty hunter was a far cry from the bounty hunter in the real life dramas of the Canadian Wild West.

The subject of bounty hunters in the Old West has long been a topic of discussion. There are those who deny such men existed and many more who are just as certain they did. The main questions appear to be these: were bounty hunters an invention of Hollywood writers striving to inject some new excitement into their screen plays? Many believe this to be the case. Were these men shadowy figures who turned in others for profit? The real picture lies some-where between.

Today bounty hunters in Canada, if indeed there are any, hold no status within the law. Wanted posters are still printed from time to time and rewards are occasionally offered and paid out, but as a profitable occupation bounty hunting disappeared from the Canadian scene nine decades ago.

Bounty hunters still operate in the United States—men and a few women who for the most part chase down bail jumpers operate legally, if not always ethically, within a wide mandate. Many are successful. Others fail. None seek publicity. Still, modern-day boun-ty hunters are far removed from the reality of the bounty hunter of the Old West.

Hollywood has always depicted the old-time bounty hunter as a nomadic, hated figure who traveled alone; and that is essentially a correct representation. The real-life bounty hunter was devoid of compassion, his only friends were his horse, his rifle (usually a Winchester) and his pistols (usually a Colt .44 or .45). He was with-out human friends, was disliked by all and feared by most. He was first and foremost a killer. His saddle bag was filled with wanted posters. He would track his quarry relentlessly; when he found him he more often than not shot the fugitive in the back. There was good reason for aiming at what came to be known as "the Texas Target"—a spot between the shoulder blades. A dead prisoner gave no trou-ble, didn't have to fed while on the trail and never escaped. Being a businessman, the bounty hunter's eye was always on overhead expenses and travel time.

How was he paid? Again Hollywood came up with an answer—a wrong one. Hollywood's bounty hunter, having run down his man, simply tied the body across the back of the outlaw's own horse or mule then took his victim to the nearest town. As he rode onto the dusty main street townspeople shrank back in contempt and revulsion as the bounty hunter and his grisly baggage passed silently. Looking neither to the right nor the left yet seeing everything, he rode directly to the sheriff's office, announced in as few words as possible that the body across the saddle was that of a wanted outlaw and asked for the reward.

The sheriff, exhibiting the same revulsion and contempt as had the townspeople, went out, looked at the cadaver, agreed that indeed it was a wanted man then motioned for the bounty hunter to reenter the office. There the sheriff dug out a locked cash-box, extracted several bills, counted them onto the desk, had him sign a receipt. Then he told him to get out of town.

The bounty hunter stuffed the bills into his pocket, walked out of the office, mounted his horse and rode silently toward the town limit quite aware that the townspeople were spitting in the dust at his departing back. He didn't care. He was already planning the pursuit of the next name on his list.

The above makes a fine screenplay but has little validity in fact.

Because of the structure of the reward systems in vogue at the time, bounty hunters were never paid cash on the spot. Sheriffs and constables never had safes full of ready cash on hand. All they could do was fill out and forward the proper papers to a higher authority. There were never any fast payments and the bounty hunter did not expect any. He had to wait for payment while the system ran its course.

The real procedures had the bounty hunter hand over the fugitive, give the authorities a mailing address and leave. The reward was paid later—by check and never quickly. The red tape involved was long, tangled and involved equal delay on either side of the border.

According to records in the archives of British Columbia (and probably also in those of the northwestern states) and in a history of the BC Police (*Policing a Pioneer Province* by Lynne Stonier-Newman, Harbor Publishing, 1991) bounty hunters were very active in B.C., Washington Territory (which included Idaho until 1890) and Montana Territory during the years between 1867 and 1900. Some were part-time hunters but quite a number were full-timers. Unfortunately, few names were ever recorded. Bounty hunters were by nature anonymous men. Anonymity meant survival.

It was during that period when cooperation between police forces, sheriffs and marshals was beginning to emerge. It was not uncommon for jurisdictions on both sides of the border to forward information on wanted men and women. This involved sharing wanted posters plus a limited granting of permission to a tracking lawman to enter the jurisdiction in his pursuit of a fugitive. Likewise, rewards were paid to lawmen who captured a wanted man from another jurisdiction. Deputies in particular depended greatly on this extra source of income.

The major problems facing lawmen on both sides of the border were the vast areas in need of policing and the usual shortage of men willing to do the dangerous job for low pay. B.C. police constables averaged $30 a month, a sheriff in Montana might make a bit more while city marshals often were hired for $1100 per year or even less. In the interior of BC, for instance, there was rarely more than one police officer assigned to an area often in excess of 12,000 square miles. As a result bounty hunters were tolerated if only because they took some of the pressure off the police. The situation in the US territories was hardly better. From 1867–70 eastern Montana was reasonably well policed but western Montana had not a single lawman, the closest marshal being in Lewiston (Idaho). In most cases an outlaw could easily escape if he had a durable horse, knew the trails and didn't arouse public interest. Most criminals who were apprehended came to grief through public cooperation with their lawmen, although sometimes, as in the cases of Henry Plummer and Boone Helm (Montana) or "One Ear Charlie" Brown (B.C.), vigilance committees did the apprehending. Such apprehension always proved fatal to the fugitive.

Because the western border between the US and Canada was rugged, unguarded and sparsely populated, it might as well not have existed. It was easy for fugitives to slip across to relative safety. Once on the "safe side" of the line, if they behaved, no one would bother them. As a result, B.C. and Alberta became home to American fugitives while Washington, Idaho and Montana became refuge for Canadians attempting to escape a similar fate. Many gave up their lawless ways, settled down and became responsible citizens. Descendants of fugitives can be found throughout the west on both sides of the border.

In many cases a fugitive was deemed by the law to be nothing worse than a nuisance so he was not pursued with any intensity. The lawmen simply waited until homesickness overcame the man. When he tried to slip back, he would be caught as was Star Child, an Alberta Indian accused of murder, who escaped to Montana. He returned a year or two later and was arrested almost immediately. He was brought to trial but, to everyone's surprise including his, was acquitted.

Others, however, were deemed dangerous or desperate enough to warrant a reward for his capture. Most rewards ranged between $100 and $300, some went as high as $500 and several offered $1,500.

One of the highest rewards offered in B.C. was $4,000 to anyone who could bring in William "Bill" Haney who, with his brother Dave and another man, had held up a train. In a shootout Dave was killed but Bill killed Isaac Decker, who had tracked the pair down. Bill Haney escaped and was never caught, although a year later a Canadian bounty hunter traced him to his parents' home in California. Bill, however, had once again fled. The trail was lost again for all time. B.C. authorities had to be satisfied that Dave had been killed by Decker in the shootout.

The northwest bounty hunters left little of substance for researchers to go on. They were men who arrived and departed without notice or fanfare. These men crossed and recrossed the border many times never reporting to anyone and never staying long in one place. Secrecy was paramount. The only time anyone might see a bounty hunter was when a lone rider brought in a prisoner. He might spend a half hour with the sheriff or police constable before riding out as quietly as he had arrived. Few would take any notice anyway for it was not a westerner's manner to ask questions of passing strangers.

There was one very important procedural difference that the bounty hunter had to consider in his pursuit. Canadian posters never mentioned "Dead or Alive." A Canadian fugitive had to be turned in alive if a reward was to be paid. If, by some chance, the fugitive was turned in dead, the bounty hunter himself could face a charge of murder or at the very least manslaughter. He would then have to convince the inquest jury that he had killed his prisoner in self defense (hard to do if the bullet had struck the deceased in the back of the head or between the shoulder blades). Regardless of the outcome he would not be paid.

In order that the majesty of the law could be upheld and

observed, the culprit had to live long enough that he could be hanged legally. Canada simply would not pay for a dead outlaw. He had to be tried and found guilty whereupon he would then either go to jail or be hanged. If he was acquitted, no reward was paid. Canadian posters contained a line in small print that read in part "...for the arrest and conviction of...." Dead was never part of the equation.

American law was not so particular. That single difference meant that American fugitives were better to pursue because their posters often made it quite clear that while alive was preferred, dead was satisfactory. However, a dead fugitive generally fetched less than one turned in alive. (Had Bob Ford been able to turn a living Jesse James over to the law, he probably would have received the full amount of the $10,000 that sat on Jesse's head. Because he elected to kill Jesse, he had to settle for less than half that amount; and he had to split it with his brother, Charlie, who had done nothing but watch and quake in fear.)

Because of this annoying difference in policy the bounty hunter, having tracked his man, was forced to make a decision that invariably depended on where the capture had taken place. If the capture took place in the United States and the quarry was Canadian he would have to take him alive. Once he had him shackled, he would turn the man over to the nearest sheriff. In these cases the sheriff notified the Canadian authorities who would send a police officer to get the fugitive and pick up the claim forms left by the bounty hunter.

The same procedure could be followed by an American bounty hunter working in Canada. However, few subscribed to this method. They were fearful the claims would be lost or stolen or the fugitive might escape on his way back to the States. Most bounty hunters held onto their prisoners and escorted them safely across the line. How many outlaws caught a bullet once they were south of the line is impossible to determine. One can only speculate that in such cases the bounty hunter had to determine if his prisoner had a reward that would justify the difference between dead and alive. It was a personal preference, one suspects.

In some cases the fugitive was wanted in Canada and Washington or Montana. In those cases the bounty hunter turned over his prisoner to the jurisdiction promising the more lucrative reward.

Bounty hunting was, after all, a business with profit the bottom line.

CHAPTER 5

The Civilian Who Humbled an Army

GABRIEL DUMONT
- ◆ b. St. Boniface, Northwest Territory, December 1837
- ◆ d. Batoche, Saskatchewan, May 19, 1906

Gabriel Dumont during his lifetime played many roles. He was born in the area of the Northwest Territories that is now southern Manitoba. He was a buffalo hunter until those animals disappeared, a plainsman, a farmer and a leader of Metis insurgents during the Northwest Rebellion of 1885 which is better known as The Riel Rebellion. Prior to and during the rebellion he was Louis Riel's principal lieutenant. Had Riel listened to him instead of his mysterious voices, he may well have emerged the victor.

Dumont was second-generation Metis. (The name given those born of French-Canadian and Native parents.) His father, Isadore Dumont, was from Quebec; his mother, Louise Laframboise, was of French and Cree blood.

Gabriel Dumont never intended to become famous. A quiet, modest, unassuming man he moved to what is now Saskatchewan where he took up farming when his buffalo hunting ended. For several years he cultivated a small acreage along the banks of the South Saskatchewan River. He augmented his farm income by running a toll ferry across the wide river. In winter he ran a trapline.

For twenty years he played the role of a farmer minding his own business and never once sought any other role in spite of ongoing entreaties from his neighbors to represent them in the continuous disputes between Ottawa and the Metis. At first he would have none of it but later saw the injustice of the federal government's policies

He eventually fell in with Louis Riel because, as did so many others, he saw Riel as the savior of the Metis. Soon, however, he became disillusioned with Riel who was beginning to show definite signs of an unbalanced mind. Because the effort of addressing the complaints of the Metis was progressing so well he stayed with him even after Riel's insanity had become apparent. Dumont took charge of a large contingent of Metis, saw to their training and use of arms and drilled them into a good enough body of soldiers that when the fighting started they acquitted themselves well. In fact, Dumont's fighters won most of their battles, made the army look foolish and, had they been a larger force, would likely have won overall. It was to Dumont's credit that he managed to mold the ragtag band into an effective fighting force.

Riel's rebellion was probably doomed from the very beginning. He had begun to make irrational statements owing to his belief that he was the reincarnation of Christ. This revelation caused a great rift among his followers, soured many of his Quebec allies and caused the Catholic Church to denounce him. Despite all that, he managed to keep a great amount of support. He eventually led the Metis and their Indian allies into tragedy when his rebellion failed against the combined force of the Canadian militia and the Northwest Mounted Police.

During the rebellion the forces under Dumont did everything but win the final skirmish. Riel, had he listened to Dumont, might have pulled off the biggest coup in the history of the Canadian west. Instead he remained indecisive, unable to give orders yet unwilling to turn command over to the one man who might have saved his followers. Dumont, in the field far removed from his commander-in-chief, could only fret silently while trying to keep his own forces motivated. Before long Riel's command collapsed and it was every man for himself. His forces scattered—all except those under the command of Dumont who fought one last, final, losing battle.

Following the failure of the rebellion Riel was captured. He went to trial in Regina. Against the advice of his lawyers who wanted to enter a plea of "not guilty by reason of insanity," Riel steadfastly refused to allow the plea. Had he done so he would likely have been acquitted. Instead he was found guilty and was hanged, November 16, 1885, at Regina.

Dumont was never arrested or prosecuted for his part in the affair. This was not an oversight on the part of Ottawa. The federal government would have scooped him up in a minute had he been available, but apprehension might have been difficult for already he was being seen for what he was—a brilliant field general, a strategist and a patriot whose only error was being on the losing side. Canadian soldiers and NWMP officers, whose duty it would have been to arrest him, respected this man, however grudging their respect may have been. Even the bumbling commander of the militia, the less-than-competent General Middleton, came to view him as a worthy opponent. In fact, Middleton was hardly a worthy opponent to Dumont who would have routed him easily had he had the resources.

Dumont, feeling he was going to be arrested, escaped to the United States. He spent some time in New York where he became a sort of celebrity much in demand as a speaker. He became famous and it may have been his international popularity that made Ottawa reluctant to push for his arrest. Dumont eventually felt safe enough to return home.

He spent the next few years trying to salvage some of the ideals for which the Metis had fought but found that even the Metis had lost interest in the original cause. In 1893 Dumont gave up the struggle and returned to his farm on the banks of the South Saskatchewan where he settled down to farm and trap once again. When he died midway through his sixty-ninth year, he had become more or less forgotten. But he did live long enough to see many of the reforms for which he had fought slowly put into law. Manitoba became a province with Saskatchewan following soon after. While the Metis never gained an independent nation, they did gain some important concessions, such as representation in political decisions and a voice in Manitoba politics. Gabriel Dumont had seen to that.

It was during the 1970s that a resurgence of interest in Riel reminded people of Gabriel Dumont. Had Riel not ignored Dumont's reasoned pleas and accepted his vision of what the Metis really wanted the rebellion would not likely have happened. Some authors and poets have hastened to glorify the mad Riel when they should have been concentrating their efforts on the sane Dumont.

However, a hanged Riel, complete with rope burns on his neck, made a better hero for tawdry apologia than did Dumont who died in his bed of old age, respected by all. Gabriel Dumont was the intelligence behind the Metis cause; Louis Riel was the catalyst that kindled its defeat.

CHAPTER 6

The Gunman Who Was Out of Date

ERNEST "ERNIE" CASHEL
- b. Buffalo, Wyoming, circa 1885
- d. Calgary, Alberta, Feb. 2, 1904

Like so many of the Old West's last badmen, Ernest Cashel was born at least thirty years too late. By the time he started his wayward career the west had changed. Lawmen were smarter and more in number, rudimentary forensic science had begun, the telegraph had made escape all but impossible, many larger centers had telephones, stagecoaches were rarely used anymore and trains had become too fast to hold up. It was Ernie's tough luck to be an 1870-style badman trying to be active in 1899.

To the citizens of the small town of Buffalo, Wyoming, the Cashel family was well known as a group of misfits although there seems to have been some sympathy for Mrs. Cashel, who by all accounts was a longsuffering woman. Mr. Cashel was a loser who could not hold a job. As a result he did little work but maybe tossed a long rope now and then although he was never caught with any rustled cattle. The three children, especially the two boys, were looked on more as nuisances than actual delinquents. That they ran wild is no real surprise for they were never heavily disciplined. The senior Cashel deserted the family shortly after the birth of his third child, a girl, never to be seen again. Mrs. Cashel supported her children by working at whatever she could get, managed to keep food, however spartan it may have been, on the table and raised her brood as well as she could, but had no success in teaching them social values beyond that of being polite when it suited their purposes. Both

John and Ernie, it was said, could charm the thorns off a rose bush and were very captivating when older women were involved.

Ernie, the middle child and second son, was the worst of the lot when it came to the wrong side of the law although his older sibling, John, came a close second. Of their sister nothing is known. She disappeared from Buffalo shortly after Ernie left and was heard from no more.

When Ernest was about fifteen, Mrs. Cashel left her unruly brood to fend for themselves and went north to her native Alberta, moved in with a sister at Ponoka, a town near Calgary, and took work as a cook in a nearby lumber camp.

The three Cashel siblings, left to their own devices, survived on petty theft until Ernest was arrested for larceny and sentenced to one year in jail. Jail didn't suit his free spirit so within days he managed to escape and fled east to Kansas. His freedom was fleeting however because on October 5, 1901, he was arrested by a U.S. marshal who recognized him from a wanted poster. The marshal telegraphed Sheriff Kennedy in Buffalo that he was holding his fugitive. Kennedy journeyed to Kansas to pick him up, but before he arrived Cashel had once again escaped.

Ernest made his way northward as quickly as his legs and a couple of stolen horses could carry him. Arriving in Alberta early in November he went directly to his mother who, although she didn't greet him with open arms, did promise to help him find work. Through her efforts he obtained work as a cowboy at John Phelan's ranch, a large spread near Sheppard, a town not far from Calgary. Phelan was satisfied with Cashel's work and told him he could stay as long as he wanted. Ernie, however, could not keep out of trouble. On October 13, 1902, he was arrested for defrauding a Calgary merchant by writing a bad check for some clothing.

Ernie, not the sharpest cactus in the desert at the best of times, was not hard to find. He had given his correct name and address when he wrote the check. He was informed by the merchant that his check had bounced but was given a few days to make the amount good. He ignored the notice. It was this oversight that eliminated any doubt that he had indeed intended to defraud the merchant who, quite rightly, went to the police and laid a complaint.

Under Canadian law, in order to obtain a guilty verdict in a fraud case the prosecutor must prove intent. The matter was fully discussed before the decision was made to go ahead with the charge. With this in mind it was decided that Ernie should be notified one more time that his check had bounced. Had Ernie offered to make good in two or three payments that would likely have settled the matter.

However, several days passed without a word from Ernie. Charges were duly laid and he was notified that a court date had been set to hear the case. He chose to ignore that as well. The judge heard the case *in absentia* finding him guilty as charged. A bench warrant was sworn out for his arrest.

The warrant was issued to a police officer from the Calgary Police Department who was sent to arrest the culprit. He had no trouble finding Ernie who was visiting his mother in Ponoka. The arresting officer hustled him aboard the next train to Calgary. Unfortunately, the officer was none too savvy in the procedures of retrieving wanted men, especially one who could turn on the charm.

On the way to Calgary, Cashel tricked the constable with the old washroom ploy. Ernie pleasantly asked the constable if he might be allowed to use the washroom, which was situated at the end of the car. The constable saw no harm in the request and removed the handcuffs. He stationed himself outside the tiny cubicle as Ernie eased inside and closed the door.

Many minutes passed. Cashel did not re-emerge. The constable knocked on the door and called out. No reply. Alarmed, the constable forced the door open to see the tiny window wide open. The slim youngster had opened the window then squeezed through to escape when the train had slowed at a siding. By the time the officer realized something was amiss his prisoner was long gone.

Cashel, having dropped from the slow-moving train without so much as a twisted ankle, had run to a nearby ranch where he stole a horse and saddle gear. With the horse under him he made good distance in a short time. Later, when he felt it safe to slow his pace, he came upon a farmer's house which he easily broke into. He stole a .44 Colt, some warm clothing and a supply of food. Following a short rest he prodded his horse along a northeast trail leading to the Mount Lake district.

Cashel, though not familiar with the Mount Lake area, managed to make his way along being very careful to avoid contact with anyone. He bypassed the town of Red Deer, caught a trail following the course of the Red Deer River and kept on that trail slowly making his way eastward. It was at this time he met a homesteader named Isaac Rufus Belt.

Belt, a naive man who kept very much to himself, had no idea of the identity of the personable young man who appeared in his farm yard one morning with a request for a bit of food and a bag of oats for his horse. Belt, who was also from the States, recognized and welcomed Cashel as a fellow American bidding him to make himself welcome. He asked for news of the outside world and Cashel told him snippets of Calgary news. Cashel made good use of the charm and soon had the homesteader offering him a job. Cashel said he was interested and after pretending to give it some thought accepted the offer.

Cashel told the homesteader his name was Bert Ellsworth, had left the States and had come to Canada in search of a challenging life. Before long Belt was completely under his spell. The unsuspecting man, elated that "Ellsworth" had accepted his offer of employment as a hired hand, told him to set up his bedroll in a corner of the sod hut—Belt's home was his home, too. Cashel pretended to settle in, did a bit of work, asked a lot of questions about the lay of the land between the Red Deer River and the northern settlements as well as what towns were along the way and their sizes and importance.

On October 31 Cashel murdered the farmer and dumped his body into the Red Deer River, cleaned the house of cash (plus a fifty-dollar gold certificate), took a shotgun, ammunition and some clothing. Saddling Belt's horse, Cashel rode northwest toward Edmonton.

This time, however, Cashel ran out of luck. Isaac Belt was not the hermit Cashel had thought he was. He had a relative living nearby whom he visited on a regular basis. Had Cashel stayed with Belt a few more days this would have become known to him and he might have altered his plans.

On November 11 Belt was reported missing by the relative. He gave the NWMP officer a good description of what Belt had in his little house including the presence of a jar that always contained a small amount of money. He also told him of the gold certificate and the livestock he owned.

The officer rode out to Belt's homestead and checked the house. He quickly noted the jar, which was now empty of money. He noted the peg on the wall where a pistol should have been and the rack that should have held a shotgun. There was no sign of the black horse, a particularly fine animal, that was well known in the territory. He also noted that if Belt had departed on his own volition he had done so without dressing appropriately. His winter gear still hung on a wall rack. His winter fleece-lined boots were neatly placed below the rack. He easily determined that foul play was likely, wrote his report accordingly and sent it off to headquarters in Calgary.

On the strength of the officer's report the NWMP assigned Constable Alec Pennycuik to the case. Pennycuik, notorious within the force for having too free a spirit and usually in trouble with his superiors over varying breaches of regulations, was a gifted investigator. So gifted, in fact, that his job was never in jeopardy despite his lack of compliance to procedure. A man of infinite patience, he would ride and reride trails, inspect and reinspect crime scenes until he had picked them clean of whatever clues they held. He would question suspects until everyone involved, including himself, was drooping from exhaustion. He never let anything distract him from the cases he was working—and he could work five and six cases at one time. His superiors, knowing how he worked even if they did not always approve of his methods, left him to his own devices and never interfered unless they had to curb his penchant for padding his expense account. They knew he would eventually settle the matter. Within an hour of receiving the report from Red Deer he began to work the case.

Cashel, meanwhile, had reached Lacombe, a town south of Edmonton. There he traded Belt's horse, saddle and bridle for a durable horse and a sturdy cart, then headed south toward Calgary.

He avoided that city by swinging off the trail heading west to cross the frozen Bow River. That put him into the Sarcee Indian Reserve where he made camp in a secluded copse of pine trees. He asked two Indian boys if they would buy him ammunition and some clothing at the trading store. The boys agreed so Cashel gave them some money telling them they could keep the change for their troubles. After the boys returned with the goods, he moved his camp further into the bush and set up a more permanent campsite.

A few days after Christmas, now calling himself Nick Carter, Cashel loaded his cart and drove to the mountains stopping along the way only long enough to steal a horse from a homestead owned by Glen Healy.

Stealing a horse he didn't need was a grave mistake. The rancher spotted Cashel in the act, but seeing the pistol hanging from the rustler's belt, was smart enough to stay hidden until the thief left. Then Healy saddled up and rode to town to report the incident. When he entered the NWMP offices by a stroke of luck the officer he encountered was Pennycuik. Healy's thorough description of the thief was enough to identify Cashel.

Meanwhile, in Lacombe, the horse trader who had dealt the dray horse and cart for the black mare noticed the saddle had the words I. R.Belt burned into the leather under a flap. At the same time he remembered having seen the horse before. He notified the Lacombe NWMP that the man he had dealt with had set out on the road to Calgary. The description was telegraphed to Calgary. It matched the one given by Healy so it was immediately forwarded to Pennycuik who sent out an all-points bulletin.

On January 24, 1903, Cashel was spotted by a patrolling Mountie at Anthracite, a small coal mining town near Banff. He immediately arrested Cashel who surrendered without incident. The officer notified Pennycuik who replied by telegraph that the officer should escort the prisoner to Calgary where Pennycuik would be waiting for him.

Cashel was thoroughly questioned about the disappearance of Belt. Naturally, he denied knowing the man. The black mare? Oh, he had bought her from a trail rider he had met. The fellow was broke and had offered her at a really cheap price.

Pennycuik knew Cashel had more to do with Belt's disappearance despite his story about buying a horse from a passing tall stranger but could do absolutely nothing with the little he had to go on. Nonetheless, he had a fair circumstantial case against Cashel and, had he chose to pursue it, might have obtained a guilty verdict in court. But the verdict would never be "...guilty of capital murder..." and that is what Pennycuik wanted. The one piece of evidence he needed was the one piece he didn't have—he had no body, a very necessary item in any murder case during that era. No body, no case. No case, no charge. Pennycuik informed the prosecuting attorney to hold off on a murder charge.

"There is a body," he told him, "and sooner or later we will find it."

"It had better be sooner, Alec," replied the prosecutor. "We can't hold this guy forever."

"We can keep him five years if the court cooperates," Pennycuik suggested. "The Healy case is cut and dried so we should proceed with it. Can you get me five years on that?"

"Dunno," the prosecutor responded. "We'll try. But the judge might decide on less."

"Go for five and settle for three," the officer said. "Something will show up. Of that I am sure."

The theft of Healy's horse was indeed cut and dried but although the prosecutor asked the judge to impose a sentence of five years Cashel's attorney presented a fine defense and argued that one year was sufficient punishment. The court split the difference and sentenced Cashel to three years in jail for stealing Healy's horse. The sentence meant that Cashel could be back on the street in two years if he behaved himself in prison but Pennycuik was not displeased. He had gained for himself some valuable working time.

In July, Belt's badly decomposed body was found snagged under a fallen tree in the Red Deer River several miles down river from his farm. The body of the unfortunate man was in such poor condition that even dragging it from the water was risky as it seemed likely to fall apart at any second. Pennycuik, as officer in charge, moved quickly. He requested, and was granted, an order that an inquest be held on the banks of the river with six hastily assembled men serving as the coroner's jury. The proceeding was extremely unpleasant for it combined an autopsy and an inquest at the same time. The heat of the day only made the procedure less appealing.

A pathologist extracted a .44-caliber bullet from the body for inspection against a slug fired from the pistol Cashel had been carrying when arrested in Anthracite. The marks on both slugs matched. (Forensic science, though in its infancy at the time, was sufficiently advanced to match rifle marks. And fingerprinting had been known since 1891.) Belt's distraught relative identified the remains by a peculiar malformation to one of Belt's legs. It was about all that was recognizable. The jury quickly agreed that this was indeed the earthly remains of Isaac Belt and that he had been killed by person or persons unknown. Pennycuik now had a body and the .44 slug to add to the evidence. He returned to Calgary to lay a charge of capital murder against Ernest Cashel.

The trial began in mid-October. It took nine days for all arguments to be heard. Cashel had a good defense lawyer who tried to sway the jury with the "possibility" that the dead body had not been that of Belt. But the jury required only thirty-five minutes to return a "guilty as charged" verdict. Cashel was sentenced to hang on December 15. Everyone thought the case was closed.

Enter John Cashel. Ernie's older brother, recently released from a Wyoming jail, had journeyed to Calgary arriving in mid-

November. Over a period of three weeks he visited Ernie every day. The two brothers talked in a small room for as long as the visiting hours allowed. Somehow, during those hours—which were supposed to be monitored—John managed to smuggle two revolvers and some ammunition to his brother one piece at a time. On 10 December, using the two revolvers, Ernie Cashel broke out of jail. He quickly escaped into the darkness and was gone.

John, however, did not flee. He either miscalculated his brother's escape date, was never told of it or felt the police would be unable to prove anything against him if he stayed put and played dumb. Whatever his reasoning, he was idling in his rooming house when the police burst in and arrested him on suspicion of aiding an escapee. John, protesting innocence, was led away.

Ernest, who could have been free for all time had he left Alberta immediately, then made yet another mistake. Instead of heading south to the relative safety of Montana he was tracked heading west into the Rocky Mountain foothills. The night he escaped he had no horse, no food, no money, no friends and did not know the land. Nonetheless, he eluded a massive search until 24 January when a posse of sixteen police officers, sixteen civilians and six soldiers caught him. Surprisingly, on the night of his escape, he had gone west only a short distance then had backtracked toward Calgary where he stayed for several days before leaving once again. When he was recaptured, he was a short distance from that city. He was hustled back to jail.

During his thirty days of freedom he had robbed two ranch houses of money and guns but even then he did not flee south. Instead, he continued to live in Calgary in a hotel room. Then he made another of his stupid mistakes. During one of his leisure days, using paper imprinted with the hotel's letterhead, he wrote a long letter to the prison chaplain. In it he gloated of his escape, stated his intentions of being around for a good many years and suggested the warden send the hangman home. The letter was turned over to Pennycuik who couldn't believe his man could be still in the area.

Cashel was smart enough to leave Calgary once he mailed his taunting letter, but still he did not head south. During the next few days tips received from various sources, plus a very reliable report that a stranger had been seen at the Pitman Ranch, indicated that Cashel was hiding on the ranch perhaps holding the owner hostage.

The aforementioned large posse under the command of Inspector Dumas, rode out to the ranch under cover of night.

All was well at the ranch house but Pennycuik and Inspector Dumas decided a thorough search of the ranch should be made. In an outbuilding they discovered a hay pile that had been used as a bed. The building was empty but a trapdoor in the floor was spotted. One of the Mounties opened it and ducked back quickly. Two bullets whizzed past his head. Cashel obviously intended to shoot it out.

Dumas called down to Cashel that the building would be burned to the ground if there was no surrender within ten seconds. Dumas began to toll down the count. Cashel meekly crawled up from the pit and surrendered his gun.

"God, boys," he said, "I don't want to be hanged and I don't want to kill any of you, but I guess I'll have to give myself up," reported the Calgary *Daily Herald*, Monday, January 26, 1904.

On February 2, 1904, Ernest Cashel was hanged at the Calgary jail. He was not yet twenty-one years old.

John Cashel was in the Calgary jail awaiting trial the day his brother was hanged. He was allowed a short, final visit. A few days later John was found guilty of abetting an escape and sentenced to a short term in jail. Upon his release he was escorted to the border and turned over to a U.S. marshal who was waiting with open arms.

At that point John Cashel disappears, as they say, from the history of the Canadian Wild West.

Ernie's longsuffering mother remained in the area cooking for many more years at various lumber camps.

Alex Pennycuik remained in the NWMP for several more years increasing his fame with more cases solved. His free spirit eventually caught up with him. In 1911, he soft-talked his superiors into authorizing a significant sum of money to enable him to follow up a major lead in one of his cases. The "lead" took him to Vancouver for two weeks then south to Seattle for another two. When he returned to Calgary, he simply reported the trip had been a failure, that the lead had been a false tip.

The story would have been accepted had Pennycuik not been seen on the coast in the best hotels and having much too good a time for someone investigating a case. The person who saw him made a report to the police force. It was obvious to his superiors that their ace detective had used police money to finance his vacation. He was discharged, in the official wording used by the force, "forthwith."

Gabriel Dumont
Without a doubt, the most competent
battle commander on either side during
the Riel Rebellion.
Photo: Courtesy of Saskatchewan Archives Board

PROCLAMATION.

ABERDEEN.

(L.S.)

CANADA.

VICTORIA, by the Grace of God, of the United Kingdom of Great Britain and Ireland, *Queen*, Defender of the Faith, &c., &c.

To all to whom these presents shall come, or whom the same may in anywise concern.— GREETING:

A PROCLAMATION.

E. L. NEWCOMBE,
Deputy of the Minister of Justice, Canada.

WHEREAS, on the twenty-ninth day of October, one thousand eight hundred and ninety-five, **COLIN CAMPBELL COLEBROOK**, a Sergeant of the North-West Mounted Police, was murdered about eight miles east of Kinistino, or about forty miles south-east of Prince Albert, in the North-West Territories, by an Indian known as "Jean-Baptiste," or "Almighty Voice," who escaped from the police guard-room at Duck Lake;

And Whereas, it is highly important for the peace and safety of Our subjects that such a crime should not remain unpunished, but that the offenders should be apprehended and brought to justice;

New Know Ye that a reward of **FIVE HUNDRED DOLLARS** will be paid to any person or persons who will give such information as will lead to the apprehension and conviction of the said party.

In Testimony Whereof, We have caused these Our Letters to be made Patent and the Great Seal of Canada to be hereunto affixed.

Witness, Our Right Trusty and Right Well beloved Cousin and Councillor the Right Honourable Sir JOHN CAMPBELL HAMILTON-GORDON, Earl of Aberdeen; Viscount Formartine, Baron Haddo, Methlic, Tarves and Kellie, in the Peerage of Scotland; Viscount Gordon of Aberdeen, County of Aberdeen, in the Peerage of the United Kingdom; Baronet of Nova Scotia, Knight Grand Cross of Our Most Distinguished Order of Saint Michael and Saint George, &c., Governor General of Canada.

At Our Government House, in Our City of Ottawa, this Twentieth day of April, in the year of Our Lord one thousand eight hundred and ninety-six, and in the Fifty-ninth year of Our Reign.

By command,

CHARLES TUPPER,
Secretary of State.

DESCRIPTION OF THE AFORESAID INDIAN "JEAN-BAPTISTE" OR "ALMIGHTY VOICE":

About twenty-two years old, five feet ten inches in height, weight eleven stone, slightly built and erect, neat small feet and hands; complexion inclined to be fair, wavey dark hair to shoulders, large dark eyes, broad forehead, sharp features and parrot nose with flat tip, scar on left cheek running from mouth towards ear, feminine appearance.

The Wanted poster issued against the renegade, Almighty Voice. Note How Closely the description matches the photo. *Photo: Courtesy of Glenbow Archives, Calgary Alberta*

Almighty Voice
This is the only photo of
Almighty Voice that exists,
but it has never been
authenticated. The subject
does, however, match official
descriptions of the renegade.
*Photo: Courtesy of the
Saskatchewan Archive Board.*

Earnest Cashel
Taken at Calgary jail just prior to his date with the hangman.
Photo: Courtesy of Glenbow Archives, Calgary Alberta

Jerry Potts

A dangerous gunfighter, scout, Indian leader and NWMP guide. Potts was as much at home with the whites as with Indians but preferred the Indian way of life.

Photo: Courtesy of National Archives of Canada (1874)

Fort Whoop-Up (1872).   *Photo: Courtesy of National Archives of Canada*

Tiny Union Bay Jail that held Henry Wagner while awaiting his transfer to Nanaimo to face a murder charge.
          Photo: Ted Meyers Collection

The Post Office in Union Bay, the last robbery for Henry Wagner before his arrest.
Photo: Ted Meyers Collection

Barkerville
Main Street as it appeared in 1865.
Photo: Courtesy of BC Archives, Province of BC

Inset: Riders prepare to leave Barkerville as guards for a
gold shipment in the summer of 1865. Some are standing
with rifles anticipating the arrival of the gold shipment.
Photo: Courtesy of National Archives of Canada

Allan McLean
The leader of the McLean gang
shown here in shackles at the
New Westminster Penitentiary.
*Photo: Compliments of the BC
Archives, Province of BC*

Archie McLean
Although deceiving by looks, Archie was a psychopathic killer and the most dangerous of the McLean gang.
Photo: Courtesy of the BC Archives, Province of BC

Charlie McLean
Taken at the New Westminster Penitentiary a few weeks before his hanging.
Photo: Courtesy of the BC Archives, Province of BC

Alex Hare
A cousin and companion of the McLean gang.
Photo: Courtesy of the BC Archives, Province of BC

The Cabin in which the McLean boys made their last stand.
Photo: Compliments of the BC Archives, Province of BC

John S. Ingram
One of the toughest lawmen either side of the border. This photo was taken when he was police chief in Calgary. *Photo: Courtesy of Glenbow Archives, Calgary Alberta*

Medicine Pipe Stem
His dalliance with Pretty Wolverine, Charcoal's 5th wife, cost him his life.
Photo: Courtesy of Glenbow Archives, Calgary Alberta.

Bad Young Man *a.k.a.* Charcoal, just a few days prior to his execution. The Stetson was given to him at his request to hide the handcuffs. The clothing was provided by the photographer.
Photo: Courtesy of Glenbow Archives, Calgary Alberta.

CHAPTER 7

The Day the Fort Was Taken

◆ FORT WHOOP-UP (Oct. 1874)

Fort Whoop-Up became the most famous of the Northwest Territories' several so-called "forts" (with names such as Robber's Roost, Whiskey Gap and Dead Horse Camp). It stood like a barrier against a backdrop of blue, cloudless sky. Its wooden palisades of sturdy pine logs reached upwards. Guard towers, higher than the walls, afforded a magnificent view of the bald prairie to all horizons. No one could approach without being seen. Not even an army of hundreds would have been able to storm across the open space between the closest copse of brush to the walls without being mowed down by the fire power that could be generated from the rifle slots in those formidable walls. Built by Montana whiskey runners, it was one of the strongest bastions ever built in the west either side of the border, the flagship of a string of forts stretching from Fort Benton, Montana, to a point just south of where stands the present-day city of Calgary.

But Whoop-Up was neither a military fort nor a symbol of civilization. Rather it represented one of the greatest evils to be visited upon the prairie Indians by white men—the dreadful plague of firewater.

Fort Whoop-Up, located at the junction of the Oldman River and the Saint Mary River not far from what is now the city of Lethbridge, Alberta, was a compound that held solid log cabins. The single entry was a massive steel gate. The fort was the northern headquarters for American whiskey runners from Montana. These entrepreneurs worked out of Fort Benton, in Montana, under the leadership of John J. Healy and Donald Watson Davis. They traded cheap whiskey, the infamous firewater, to Indians for valuable furs. The enterprise thrived and remained in operation for several years before the Canadian government, finally aware of the negative impact on the Natives, decided something had to be done about the situation.

On July 8, 1874, a large detachment of NWMP officers under command of Inspector George Arthur French headed westward from Dufferin, Manitoba, on a long trek across the unmapped prairie. Inspector French, aware that Fort Whoop-Up was a heavily armed stockade, felt the need for a vast amount of equipment and a large force of Mounties. As is usual with bureaucrats, he took far too much equipment of the wrong type. The horses he chose, fine thoroughbreds from eastern stables, quickly showed themselves unsuited to the harsh country.

Accompanying the 275 officers and men were 73 wagons and 114 Red River ox carts all loaded to over capacity with supplies and ammunition. (A Red River cart was a wooden wagon with two very high wheels, ideal for deep ruts. Made entirely of wood, the axles made a loud screeching howl that could run shivers down anyone's back until they got used to the sound.) A herd of ninety-three steers for slaughter was strung out behind the wagons. Included in the equipment were mowing machines to cut fodder for the horses, oxen and cattle, two nine-pound field guns, two brass mortars, several field kitchens and several portable forges. The overall columns trailed for more than two miles.

The march did not go well from the onset. There was squabbling between the policemen and the civilian guides (none of whom were qualified as time was to prove). The black flies and mosquitoes were at their worst. Hordes of millions of grasshoppers periodically descended upon the column. In one such scourge the grasshoppers ate all the fodder in the hay wagons and then denuded the wagons of paint as well. Then the weather turned bad.

Thunderstorms, called "blue northers" by prairie folk, spooked the cattle and the resulting stampede scattered the animals over a vast area. The men were not cowboys and had no idea of what to do in such an event. By the time they rounded up the herd, a task that took nearly a week, they discovered many were missing—Indian hunting parties had found them first.

The prairie storms were something none of the force had ever encountered. Men and beasts were bombarded by hailstones the size of walnuts. The rains, which occurred in series, disrupted the march time and time again. Once the columns got underway following each storm, the cattle and supply wagons proved unable to keep up with the normal gait of the still-spirited horses. As a result, supper was often hours late and in some cases nonexistent. The water wagons were often nowhere in sight.

In August, French was forced to allow several wagons and some sick men to return to Manitoba. By September they were still in Saskatchewan. (Although in 1874 there was no province of Saskatchewan, the author uses this term to help the reader identify the area in which the force was lost.) The guides were totally out of their element and the flat prairie offered no landmarks. The troop became hopelessly lost. The police, bewildered and exhausted, stopped to regroup.

Then the fine, spirited eastern horses began to give out. Unable to adapt to the rigors of the prairie they simply quit. Some of the men had found tough western mustangs along the way and these animals kept the riders mobile.

French, uncertain of his next move, decided to head for country he knew and pushed south toward Fort Benton, Montana. (Montana was not yet a state, but the term enables the reader to better identify the geographic position.) There he knew he could find supplies and hoped he might perhaps find a qualified guide. He was also well aware that he was outside his jurisdiction, that the Sioux were hostile and that the Americans would resent the presence of foreign policemen in their lawless midst. French, however, felt the risks warranted the decision. Leaving the main body of his troop, he and a selected few rode south into Montana.

At Fort Benton fate intervened in the form of Jerry Potts, an enigmatic scout who answered in monosyllables and then only if he had to speak at all. French hired the strange gunfighter as a guide. Ironically it was D. W. Davis, the very man French intended to put out of business, who recommended Potts as a guide.

French left Fort Benton with replenished supply wagons and a string of mustangs to replace the eastern horses who had proven themselves so useless. Potts guided the troopers back to the main force with unerring accuracy.

Back in Saskatchewan French split his large force into two groups. He sent Inspector James MacLeod (with Potts) on to Alberta with the healthiest men, now all astride the feisty mustangs, the cannon and mortars plus adequate supplies in wagons pulled by sturdy dray horses. French said his goodbyes to MacLeod then moved northeast toward a small outpost called Swan Lake with the carts, oxen, the remaining horses and the unhealthy men.

MacLeod's group, under the expert guidance of Jerry Potts, quickly located Fort Whoop-Up. On October 9, a crisp, cool morning, the troop crested a rolling hill. There in front of them loomed the fort in all its sinister glory—a daunting sight. MacLeod scouted out the area. What he saw both impressed and worried him. He could see no movement behind the forbidding walls. In fact, the place looked so deserted MacLeod smelled a trap and acted accordingly.

Figuring he was in for a tough fight he deployed his force out of rifle range (about 500-700 yards). Then he ordered the two nine-pounders and the mortars be brought forward. These were set up where they could be seen, the mortars elevated to allow their shot to clear the wall and land within the enclosure while the cannons were trained directly on the massive steel gate.

MacLeod allowed enough time for anyone within the fort to take a good look at the cannon. Then, carrying a white flag of truce, he and Potts rode toward the palisades. When they came to the massive gate Potts hammered on it with his rifle butt. Slowly the gate swung open and MacLeod was somewhat surprised to be greeted by an elderly man who extended his right hand in a gesture of friendship. The two men shook hands and the old man invited the Mountie and Potts to enter. MacLeod, not without apprehension accompanied the elderly one into the fort.

"Name's Dave Akers," said the old man. "Been expectin' you."

"Are you the owner of this place?" replied MacLeod.

"Sure am. C'mon in," Akers waved toward the main building. "Yer jest in time for some supper. Hope yer likes buffalo."

There was another man inside, a fellow who said his name was Conrad. He also extended his hand to MacLeod. Over supper MacLeod asked Akers once again if he owned the fort. Akers replied again in the affirmative. MacLeod already knew (or at least suspected) the true owner was I. G. Baker of Montana but had to catch Akers in his lie. He offered to purchase the fort on behalf of Canada for ten thousand dollars. Akers, caught off guard, did not know what to do. Obviously Baker had not prepared him for such a circumstance. He looked across to Conrad who MacLeod had correctly assumed to be Baker's real agent. Conrad shook his head ever so slightly but MacLeod spotted it. Now he knew his surmise had been correct so he played his next ace.

"Very well, then," he said, addressing Conrad more than Akers, "I hereby confiscate this structure in the name of the Canadian government."

There was no reaction from either man.

"I must also inform you," he continued, "that I am authorized by Ottawa to stamp out the whiskey trade in this territory and to try all runners who are captured. Those I find guilty will be hanged."

At this point the Mountie rose from the table, thanked Akers for the fine supper of buffalo stew, told the two men he would allow them a couple of hours to collect their belongings and clear out and strode to the gate. He beckoned his troop forward.

Fort Whoop-Up had been taken without a shot being fired. It passed from its phase as flagship of the Montana whiskey runners to its phase as temporary headquarters for the NWMP. Its passing into police hands spelled the beginning of the end of the whiskey trade in the Canadian Northwest Territory.

Inspector MacLeod knew the structure was just the ticket for his winter camp and he used it until the completion of new buildings a few miles further north. The new fort was named Fort MacLeod, as chosen by members of MacLeod's force, and around it grew a large town which in turn became known as MacLeod.

Inspector MacLeod turned his men quickly to revamping Fort Whoop-Up for police use. They first revised and remodeled the buildings within for use as winter shelters and as soon as that work was completed they moved, in a series of quick raids, against the whiskey traders.

In the first raid they arrested William Bond, one of the chief traders, and four of his accomplices. The police confiscated two wagons filled with brimming whiskey kegs, sixteen horses, many rifles, pistols and a great number of hides and furs. Bond watched as his whiskey was poured onto the ground. He howled in anguish as his furs and hides were doled out to nearby Indians and he watched in sullen hatred as his horses were led into the police stables. He and his cohorts were then fined up to $200 each.

Unable to pay the fines, the five men were put to work chopping wood and mucking out stables until an American merchant named J. D. Weatherwax arrived from Fort Benton with funds to bail the men out. Bond, however, had managed to escape and was never seen again in Canada.

Weatherwax, railing against the injustice of Canadian law, paid the fines and rode off. However, a few days later he, too, was arrested when a patrol found him and a man named Diamond R. Brown trading whiskey to Indians. A huge cache of whiskey, furs, hides, rifles and pistols were confiscated. Brown and Weatherwax were each fined $240.

Weatherwax blustered and threatened to bring all the force of Washington down upon the Canadians' heads but his threats made no impression on MacLeod. Instead, Weatherwax spent two weeks cutting wood and cleaning stables until friends in Montana arranged for the fines to be paid. He, too, left Canada never to return.

Aside from an angry editorial in the Fort Benton Record, by John J. Healy, leading whiskey merchant and the paper's editor, no complaint from Washington ever materialized. Healy, enraged when his own whisky enterprise was smashed by the NWMP, angrily editorialized:

"We know from experience [about the heavy-handed Canadian laws], but we had no idea that the persons and property of American citizens would be trifled with."

Meanwhile, one by one, the other forts in the chain were being seized and destroyed. All confiscated furs, rifles and food were given over to Natives.

Fort Whoop-Up still stands but is in ruins. There are plans afoot to restore it to its original appearance as a tourist attraction.

CHAPTER 8

Badman from Tombstone

FRANK SPENCER
- b. Tennessee, circa 1857
- d. Kamloops, B.C., July 1890

Frank Spencer, who should not to be confused with a more famous Arizona outlaw Pete Spence, went west to Texas from his childhood home in Tennessee when he was sixteen. He was a tough kid but was not yet the outlaw he would become. He quickly found work on a cattle ranch and worked as a ranch hand for a while before leaving for another ranch as a drover on a spring cattle drive. Drovers earned more than those who stayed behind to mend fences and do yard work, but of course the work was harder and the conditions were worse. Apparently he was good with horses and stayed with the new outfit at least three years.

When he was twenty, he made his final drive, this time to Dodge City. He liked Dodge so much he decided to stay awhile. Whether he worked in Dodge or not is unknown but he may have tried his luck at the card tables as a gambler. If that was the case, he was never colorful or successful enough to make a splash. His anonymity was probably a good thing for this was during the time "Mysterious Dave" Mather was a city constable. Mather was not an example of a good lawman, but he was very fast with his gun and therefore had little trouble keeping order in that restless town. Spencer had a temper and was given to making rash moves, so he was very smart not to have pushed against "Mysterious Dave" during his Dodge City days.

That Spencer never tangled with Mather is a fact attested to by his remaining alive, but he did have a couple of minor brushes with the law and spent some time, likely the usual thirty days, in jail. When he was released, he decided that Dodge was not his kind of town after all so he boarded a stage one morning and headed west once again. This time the trail led to Tombstone, Arizona.

His arrival in that wicked town, during 1878, made no impression on anyone, so again his initial occupation remains unknown. Eventually, however, he decided to put his ranching skills to work and found a spot on the ranch owned by Newman "Old Man" Clanton and his sons, Ike, Phen and Billy. (Billy was killed in the OK Corral shoot-out. Ike was shot and killed by a deputy sheriff and Phen died in prison.) If Frank didn't know from the outset that the Clanton ranch dealt mainly in rustled cattle he soon found out. Obviously the knowledge didn't bother him because he stayed on with Old Man Clanton and rode with the gang for more than two years.

Obviously he got along well with his compadres, notorious fellows such as Johnny Ringo, Curly Bill Brocius, Billy Claibourne, the aforementioned Pete Spence and several others. He probably had a nodding acquaintance with Wyatt Earp and his brothers as well as "Doc" Holliday and probably knew "Buckskin Frank" Leslie as well for Leslie worked in the Oriental Saloon, a place Spencer would have frequented during his trips to town.

In August, 1881, Old Man Clanton and some of his riders were ambushed and killed in Guadeloupe Canyon. Frank was not with them that fateful day but was possibly spooked by the event because he left hurriedly for Montana. There he engaged in rustling with "Dutch" Henry's gang until 1886, the year the Stock Growers' Association, under the leadership of a rancher called "Strangler" Stuart, made things too hot for rustlers. (Granville Stuart later became an author and also served as a U.S. senator for Montana. The name Strangler came from the number of rustlers he and his vigilantes hanged.) Henry and the gang quickly dispersed to various points of the compass. Frank Spencer decided to head north to safer pastures.

Spencer went into that part of the Northwest Territory that is now Alberta, worked honestly at a ranch south of Calgary for a few months then crossed the Rockies into B.C. He ended up near Kamloops where he found work on the Campbell Ranch, a large spread. Had he behaved himself he would have been able to stay at the ranch for many years as the management liked his way with horses. They were not so enamored of his quick temper and worried that he made such little effort to keep it under control. As it was, he managed to stay coolheaded for almost a year.

In 1887 Frank and a fellow cowpoke named Pete Foster were spending a day off drinking in the bunk house. They got into an argument over the ownership of a bottle of "red eye" whiskey, an argument that became more heated with the passing minutes. Spencer finally accused Foster of stealing the bottle from his bunk box whereupon Foster shouted that Spencer didn't know what he was talking about. The accusations led to pushing. The combatants pushed and shoved their way out of the bunk house across the yard into the corral. Foster was clearly winning the fracas when Spencer reverted to his old habits. He drew his .45 Colt and shot the unarmed Foster directly in the chest. The stricken man pitched face down into the dirt. Within a few seconds he lay dead in the dust of the corral.

Realizing what he had done Spencer quickly sized up the situation. His only recourse was to take flight so he leapt to the saddle of a horse that was awaiting its rider. The horse was fully equipped with saddle bags containing food and clothing. The saddle holster held a rifle. Frank Spencer reined the horse toward the gate, jabbed his boot heels into the mustang's rib cage and before anyone could react was racing at a full gallop down the road away from the ranch.

Because of the time it took to inform the police at Kamloops of the killing, Spencer had a long jump on the lawman assigned to find him. The officer, a B.C. police constable named Walter Smith, was a veteran man-hunter who had brought in several fugitives over the years. Smith and two Native trackers set out on the trail as soon as possible. Smith, although he felt the time lapse to be too great, kept doggedly on the easily followed trail hoping that Spencer might grow careless or perhaps get lost in the bush and begin to travel in circles. Smith's hopes were not to be. The trail continued due south.

After a three-day ride Smith and his trackers came to the border and the realization that Spencer had crossed into the comparative safety of Washington. Even at that he was only a few hours ahead of the pursuers who had closed the gap considerably. In all likelihood, had Smith been able to contact the American authorities, he might have nabbed his man. At the time, however, the telegraph was not yet installed in the still very remote area.

Smith returned to Kamloops and sent out wanted posters to all points and to Washington Territory authorities. The posters contained only a description for no pictures of Spencer were available. Nonetheless, the description was so good one of those posters eventually brought Spencer to justice.

Frank Spencer did not stay in Washington any longer than it took him to ride to the Oregon boundary. He probably feared the B.C. authorities might convince their Washington counterparts to permit the man hunters he knew would be on his trail to continue the chase. He wisely kept going until he was well into Oregon. There he felt safe and began looking for work.

He soon hired on as a handler for a prominent horse breeder and again might have spent the rest of his life free as a bird. His skills with horses quickly made a good impression on his new boss, so much so that he was soon being treated as one of the family. Spencer never spoke of his past but he did tell his boss, without going into details, that he had run into a bit of trouble in Canada.

The years slipped by with Spencer feeling safer each passing day. On his trips to Pendleton he had always made a habit of checking the sheriff's office notice board to see if he might turn up on one of the wanted posters that occasionally was tacked up. None ever appeared and after three years had come and gone he discontinued the practice. He began to feel he had been forgotten. His confidence was too optimistic, however, for the day came that he allowed himself a very serious error in judgement.

One morning in 1890 the ranch owner visited the bunk house asking if anyone would like to accompany some horses he was shipping by rail to a ranch near New Westminster, B.C. Frank said he would go. The breeder, remembering that Spencer had been in some sort of trouble north of the border, warned him off saying such a trip would be taking too great a risk. His warning words proved to be prophetic.

"Up there in Canada, Frank," he told him, "the law only gives you one shake of the dice."

Spencer shrugged off the warning. Three years was a long time, the trouble had been in Kamloops, more than 250 miles northeast of New Westminster, and he was actually known to only a handful of people, certainly less than a dozen. He felt safe. He would go with the horses. The breeder reluctantly gave approval. After all, he may have thought, Frank might be right and if a man is foolish enough to defy the fates then let him do it.

Spencer oversaw the herding of the horses aboard the freight car then went to a passenger car and settled in for the travel to New Westminster.

Upon arrival in New Westminster he disembarked his horses and turned them over to the new owner who was waiting with enough wranglers to herd them to his ranch. The owner declined Frank's offer to ride with them much to Frank's delight. He would be able to spend the night in the city, see a variety show that a poster advertised was being staged in a local opera house, visit a saloon then get a good night's sleep before catching the next morning's train south. (In the old west an opera house had nothing to do with opera. They were variety theaters often attached to a saloon.) Spencer checked into a hotel, asked about the stage show, then wandered down the street to a saloon for a drink before supper.

His drink had not even arrived when Spencer felt the presence of someone standing beside him.

"You are Frank Spencer, are you not?" the stranger asked, quietly.

"Yes, I am," Frank replied.

"I am Constable Isaac Decker of the B.C. Police Force," the stranger said. "I am informing you that I am arresting you for the murder of Peter Foster in Kamloops."

Spencer, confused, bewildered and not knowing what else to do, went along quietly. He had every right to be confused. No doubt he asked the constable how he knew him. Isaac Decker would have replied that he didn't know him, he had identified him from an old wanted poster.

The fates work in mysterious ways. Decker happened to be in New Westminster by mere chance. He was the police constable in the small town of Ashcroft, more than 220 miles of rough trail north of New Westminster. His trip to New Westminster had been his first in more than two years. He had never seen Spencer nor did he know anyone who had. He had never been to Kamloops and didn't know anyone there, either. So how had he recognized Spencer from a wanted poster he had only glanced at three years before? The poster had no photo but might as well have had for Smith, the original tracker, was a stickler for detail.

Not even the smallest, most insignificant item was ever overlooked when Smith put together a wanted poster. If a suspect had a dimple in his chin or a wart on his index finger, the fact would find its way into his descriptive narrative. As a result of Smith's devotion to detail, the posters that originated in Kamloops had been very well detailed. Besides giving the usual estimates of appearance, age, height and complexion Smith had included that the suspect spoke with a distinctive American drawl generally associated with the deep south and that he was missing a finger.

The two lawmen, who did not know each other, had combined to place Spencer at the short end of the odds. Smith's insistence on detail had merged with Decker's photographic memory.

Constable Decker had come to New Westminster from Ashcroft to attend a trial and give evidence. The trial had ended that afternoon, the jury had returned its verdict and the judge had adjourned the court. His day over, Decker had changed to civilian clothing from his uniform and gone to the saloon for a cool beer before going back to his hotel for supper and good night's sleep. Morning would come early for him as he was to catch the early stagecoach for the long, tiring trip back to Ashcroft. He certainly had no idea his long day would end with his apprehension of a fugitive.

Decker had taken his pint of ale to a table and was sitting with his back to the wall watching the patrons. His trained eyes casually scanned the crowd as the patrons came and went. He had seen the tall, lean young man enter the saloon, had noted the way he glanced here and there in the manner of a man unfamiliar with the surroundings and quickly pegged him as a visitor. He paid no further attention as the stranger crossed to the long bar, placed his left foot on the brass rail, fished in his jacket pocket for some cash then waited for the bartender who was busy at the far end of the bar. Decker turned his attentions to another part of the saloon and would not have given the fellow another look had his interest not suddenly been reawakened.

When the man ordered his drink, he did so in the rich accent of a man from the American west. Americans were no strangers to the Canadian southwest but Decker took a closer look more through force of habit than anything else. When he noticed the hand with the absent finger, a tiny bell rang in his mind. His memory began to flash through the wanted posters he had mentally filed away. And the name Frank Spencer leaped out at him. He rose quietly from his chair and sidled up to the young man being very careful not to spook him.

The following morning Decker canceled his seat on the stage.

Instead he appeared in court to tell the judge how—and why—he had arrested Frank Spencer. Spencer was quickly remanded in custody until arrangements could be made for him to be returned to Kamloops for trial. Decker caught the Ashcroft stage the following day.

Two weeks later, in handcuffs and under escort, Frank Spencer began his return journey to Kamloops. In late March his trial for the murder of Pete Foster began. In the custom of the day the trial was quick. Prosecution stated its case, defense stated its case, the judge made his summation pointing out to the jury points of law that had to be considered, the jury retired to consider the evidence and then returned to give the verdict. Most murder trials lasted two days. Frank Spencer's took three.

With the verdict of guilty duly recorded the judge intoned the mandatory sentence of death by hanging. In those days of swift, uncompromising justice no other sentence was possible. The sentence could be reduced to life in prison but that was strictly the bailiwick of the Court of Appeals. Spencer's appeal was duly dismissed and forty days later, Frank Spencer, the Tombstone badman was hanged.

Spencer was, however, granted his final request. For reasons which he did not divulge he asked that he be permitted to wear slippers to the gallows. He simply said he did not want to die with his boots on. The request was granted.

It has since been speculated that Frank Spencer had made a promise to his mother that he would not die with his boots on, the phrase being a euphemism for dying violently. It was a promise a genteel southeastern mother might extract from a son prior to his departure for the rough life in the western territories.

Isaac Decker left the police force a few years later and bought a ranch. In June of 1909, almost twenty years after he had arrested Frank Spencer, he received a request to accept a temporary appointment as special constable. His tracking skills were wanted in hunting down two men believed to have been two-thirds of a gang that had robbed a train. He agreed and joined a small group that eventually picked up the trail near the Thompson River. Decker, figuring he could get a lead on the fugitives, rode several miles ahead then set up a stakeout at a bend in the river.

Shortly Decker spotted a boat with two men approaching. The men steered the boat to shore a few yards from where Decker was hiding. He drew his gun as the men, unaware they were being watched, left the boat and walked in his direction. As they drew near Decker realized that one of the men had a pistol in his hand. He also realized the two had seen him.

Decker fired. The .45 slug struck the man directly on the chin and slammed into his head. He fell and died within seconds. His companion, however, snapped off one shot a split second after Decker had fired. Decker died where he fell, a bullet through his heart. His killer escaped into the woods. An Indian woman who had been gathering berries witnessed the shoot-out. She gave evidence at the ensuing inquest.

The dead man was later identified as Dave Haney, an outlaw from California. The man who had escaped was his brother, Bill. Despite the combined efforts of lawmen on both sides of the border Bill was never caught. Neither was the third man of the original trio.

CHAPTER 9

The Photogenic Outlaw

JAMES GADDY
- ◆ b. Manitoba, 1861
- ◆ d. June 13, 1888

Jim Gaddy was born in the Qu'Appelle Valley, a beautiful area of wooded, rolling hills and lush glens that stretch from the northwest section of Manitoba westward into what was then called the Northwest Territories, but is now Saskatchewan. According to one legend the area got its name when a French explorer, astounded by the valley's natural beauty asked, quite innocently, "Qu'appelle? [What is this called?]." The Cree guide replied he did not know if the valley had a name so it was decided to let the question name the valley and the river that flows through it. The legend may or may not be true.

Gaddy probably never dwelt on the beauty of the valley that was his home because his childhood was one of poverty and hard times. It was made worse because he was Indian in a country that no longer had anything to offer the first nations of the land. His people had been herded into a reservation in the expectations that they would remain compliant children of the Great White Mother across the sea. With their traditional hunting and trapping areas no longer open to them, there was no viable source of income and no industry in the area that might have offered employment. As a result, Jimmy Gaddy became a wild kid—not totally out of control but not all that compliant either.

Young Jimmy went from one minor scrape to another until he was ten years of age. From that age onward, his behavior became progressively worse until the law became fully involved. Usually, the Mounties picked him up without fuss and hauled him into the juvenile division of what passed for a court system. There a magistrate (often an NWMP inspector) would sentence him to a period of probation and release him to his parents.

Unfortunately, his parents had long since lost interest in him and neither they nor Jimmy understood or cared about the white man's legal system. By the time he was seventeen, in 1878, he was, if not a professional thief, at least an enthusiastic amateur. The following year he stole some horses from a nearby ranch but was caught when he tried to sell them to a man who was actually a visiting police officer. He was arrested, found guilty and sent to jail for five years.

His behavior in prison was such that he earned not a single day of good behavior remission and the authorities kept him behind bars for his full term. Released in 1884 he behaved himself and may even have intended to lead an honest life. Then early in 1887 he met up with Moise Racette, a man he had befriended in jail. The two worked at odd jobs here and there in Manitoba and Saskatchewan but were always short of money. Still, neither man seems to have had intentions of returning to his former life as a criminal.

At this point a strange quirk of fate intervened. An itinerant photographer from Winnipeg named Allen Sutherland set up a tent in the town of Qu'Appelle for the summer. Photography was new to the west and getting one's picture taken had become all the rage. Cowboys, city folk, outlaws, lawmen, gamblers, prostitutes and politicians flocked to studios to pose for portraits. City women would dress in all their finery, most men wore their best suits, lawmen were careful to display their star or badge of office while outlaws and cowboys alike invariably posed with their favorite rifles and pistols. A photographer could make a better-than-average profit during the summer by traveling here and there with a tent studio then return to a city studio for winter sittings.

In May Racette and Gaddy visited Sutherland's tent and were photographed together. They were issued a numbered card and informed they could pick up the prints in two days. The procedure at the time was to pay for the pictures (about one dollar each) when they were picked up. The only problem facing Gaddy and Racette was that neither had a dollar and were unlikely to have any two days hence.

However, they wanted the pictures and were determined to get money somewhere. They decided to venture far afield, steal a horse and sell it to some horse trader who wouldn't ask questions. They would have enough money then to buy their photos and have a small surplus to boot. A good horse in those days sold for $75 although the trader's buying price would never exceed $30—much less if the trader had suspicions that the horse might have been corralled by a long rope (rustled).

That night the pair strapped their revolvers to their belts, saddled their horses and made their way to Moose Jaw, a small town some distance southwest, a good two or three days' ride from the Qu'Appelle Valley. Camping not far from town, they waited quietly during the rest of the day then made a night visit to a homestead. There they stole two ponies and a good horse. With their booty in tow the pair hightailed it north. What they did not know was that the homestead belonged to a man named Hector McLeish.

McLeish was not a man to trifle with. He had been in the west for years and subscribed to the philosophy that the meek were not likely to inherit the earth other than a six-by-three-by-six grave. McLeish was not a meek man. He wanted his share while he was alive to enjoy it.

When McLeish noticed his animals missing, he knew right away they had been stolen. Two unaccountable sets of hooves plus footprints from two pairs of strange boots told the story plainly enough. He called on a friend and the two saddled up, checked their rifles and set out on the search. They tracked their quarry to a point a few miles from Qu'Appelle at which point the tracks suddenly turned west—toward central Saskatchewan.

McLeish and his companion rode into town and introduced themselves to the local law officer, Sgt. Tyffe of the NWMP. Tyffe and some townsmen decided to accompany McLeish and his friend. The posse easily picked up the trail and spent the next two days tracking. Along the way they gained valuable information from settlers who had seen two riders leading two ponies and a horse. The information made it much easier for the posse to determine the direction the culprits were heading.

On the second day a settler gave a detailed description of one of the riders. Tyffe immediately realized the settler was describing Moise Racette. The Mountie opined that Racette and his still unknown companion were heading for Racette's hometown, a place called Wolseley. They spurred their horses forward on Tyffe's hunch.

The posse arrived in Wolseley about 10:30 p.m. on May 30 and conferred with town police officer Constable Mathewson. Mathewson informed the posse that Racette would likely be at his family's homestead, a small holding not far from town. The possemen then retired to the Pritchard Hotel intending to deal with their quarry the following morning. McLeish and Mathewson decided to check out the homestead as it was only a mile from town.

As they neared the farm, they saw Racette saddling a horse. Realizing he was going to ride out, the pair decided to act without the assistance of the posse. They rode into the farmyard, rifles at the ready.

Mathewson easily arrested Racette but at that moment Gaddy ran from the house toward the corral. McLeish stopped him but failed to notice a third man (he turned out to be Racette's father) come from the house. He leapt on Mathewson's back. The force of the blow caused the constable to drop his revolver.

Gaddy shook loose from McLeish, seized the pistol and fired three shots into McLeish. Realizing what he had done, he dropped the pistol and surrendered to Mathewson. Racette had also lost his bravado and he too surrendered. The two helped carry the wounded McLeish into the house then offered to ride into Wolseley for the town doctor. Mathewson was having none of that but knew McLeish needed quick attention. He decided his best option was to leave McLeish in the farmhouse and ride the mile to town for a doctor. He ordered both prisoners to saddle up and ride with him.

Gaddy, meanwhile, had regained his composure. He managed to conceal a small pistol in an inside pocket of his jacket. As the three galloped toward town he turned in the saddle and took a shot at the policeman. He missed and Mathewson spurred his horse forward, dragged Racette off his horse and was wrestling him to submission when Gaddy took two more shots at the Mountie. Both merely grazed his uniform but the two prisoners now had the upper hand. They forced Mathewson to return to the farm, ordered him not to leave until the sound of their horses had receded and rode into the darkness.

Mathewson immediately rode for town and returned with the doctor who patched McLeish up enough for a buggy ride to town. McLeish, however, was beyond help and died at 8:40 a.m. the following morning.

The posse of angry riders searched the area for days but neither

Racette nor Gaddy were seen, and it soon became apparent they had managed to escape into Montana. To this point still no one knew the identity of Racette's companion and the trail was growing colder by the day. A warrant for the arrest of the pair was issued. Posters offering a reward of $500 were duly printed and distributed throughout the area and sent south of the border.

Meanwhile, Allen Sutherland, having photographed nearly everyone in the area, had closed his tent studio and returned to Winnipeg. When he read of the murder, the descriptions given brought to mind the two men who had come to him to have their picture taken. He had wondered why they had never come back to pick up the photos. They had both seemed so eager, almost childlike in their excitement.

Sutherland retrieved the photos from his files and took the prints to the NWMP office. The viewing officers had no trouble identifying Racette and a check with prison authorities subsequently identified Gaddy. New posters bearing copies of the picture were printed and sent to lawmen including those south of the border. (Unfortunately, none of the photos appear in any archives. It seems they were either lost or destroyed.)

On August 12 Sheriff Lou Beck of Lewiston, Montana, accompanied by a deputy, was visiting Fort McGinnis when he noticed two men hanging around the fort's trading post. He recognized both men from the picture on the recently arrived posters. He called his deputy to cover him then arrested both men. Following a few questions the men admitted they were Gaddy and Racette. The NWMP was quickly notified. The return telegram requested Beck hold the pair. Mathewson, now a corporal, traveled by stage to Lewiston, identified the suspects, served the warrant and shackled the two prisoners for the long trip to Wolseley. Before he left, he handed Sheriff Beck a check for the $500 reward.

James Gaddy was arraigned in custody pending his trial. The case against him was open and shut so great was the evidence. A surprise witness against him was Peter Gaddy, his brother. Peter testified he had been at the Racette farm the night of the killing and had seen the entire episode. He gave a clear account of the proceedings that fateful night.

The jury received the case following instructions from the judge and retired to consider their verdict. They returned in less than two hours. The verdict was "guilty as charged." The judge intoned the mandatory death sentence and James Gaddy was led back to his cell.

Jimmy Gaddy, tough kid and small-time horse thief, had only wanted to own his photograph. He did not turn to murder until after he had fallen under the influence of a tougher man. He was hanged at Regina on the morning of June 13, 1888. He was twenty-seven years of age.

Had it not been for the urge to pose for a photograph he could not afford, he would have remained at large for a long time. After all, the only man identified had been Racette and no one had even considered Gaddy as a suspect. He had been the "person unknown." Perhaps he would never have been caught.

Racette on the other hand did not hang. He escaped from jail just days before his trial was to begin. He was tracked once again to Montana, was actually seen, but then disappeared into the western mountains before further action could be taken. Obviously he took great care to avoid Lewiston for he was never seen again. One story, fairly well substantiated, has it that he wintered with a band of Lakotas in a mountain village. In the spring of 1889 he departed and was last seen riding south toward Utah.

CHAPTER 10

The Trouble with Isaac

ISAAC MONTGOMERY BARR
* b. Hornby, Ontario, March 2, 1847
* d. Australia, 1937

Isaac Barr was a dreamer. As a youngster in the small Ontario town of Hornby he dreamed of many things, but his greatest dream was to become a world-famous minister. His family was religious—at least his mother was—so he was drawn toward the faith. The thought of being a minister was never far from his young mind.

He was also a child who loved adventure, so it was natural that he spent much of his time exploring the woods and river banks of the area in which he lived. He read books of adventure and was enthralled by the adventures of Daniel Boone and the early woodsmen who roamed the woods of North America. By the time he was eighteen, though, the religious calling had him pretty well hooked. He informed his family that he wished to become a minister. His father was agreeable; his mother was delighted.

Isaac went away to a prestigious theology college in Toronto and was duly ordained as a minister in the Anglican Church. He was pleased when he received a position in a parish in England. He embarked aboard a British ship and arrived in England and his new parish several weeks later.

The Reverend Isaac Barr, however, soon realized his sense of adventure was not going to leave him. Within a few years he was hankering for Canada and a chance to go to the western territory that was only beginning to develop. Still, he had come to love the English people he dealt with so he was torn between loyalty to them and his desire for adventure. How could he have both sides of a good thing, he wondered? The answer, as they say, came to him as in a vision. He would not only go to western Canada he would take as many of his flock as possible with him. He, Isaac Barr, would establish an English settlement in the heartland of that great prairie. More years passed as he considered it. The more he pondered, the more he decided the idea had great merit.

He was about forty-seven years of age when he began to seriously pore over a large map of what is now Saskatchewan and Alberta. The fact that the map was poorly surveyed caused him no worries whatsoever. After all, there were already a couple of cities established in the vast expanse of prairie. He would choose one as a base of operations and go from there.

By 1898, now aged fifty-one, he was ready to make his pitch. Using his pulpit as a soapbox the Reverend Isaac touted his scheme for establishing an English settlement colony in Canada along the banks of the North Saskatchewan River. He must have been very persuasive for he received many enquiries about his proposal. In fact his project attracted many more applicants than he had envisioned. Perhaps the vast numbers involved should have given him misgivings but he signed them all up and journeyed to Canada to make arrangements for the movement of some 2,000 people to a new home on the bald prairie.

Reverend Barr may have been a first-class minister but his management skills soon proved so lacking that his advanced planning ended up being poor to the extreme. He arrived in Ottawa and sought out the proper department where he made his proposal to a clerk. The clerk referred him to his supervisor and an appointment was set up for a more formal presentation. Barr made his presentation then sat back awaiting a decision. The bureaucrat told Barr there might be substance in the proposal and agreed such a settlement might prove suitable for a site along the North Saskatchewan River.

"Leave your proposal with me," the bureaucrat said, "and I will look into it."

Isaac was so naive about the workings of governments that he understood the statement "I'll look into it" to mean his request for a huge tract of land large enough to accommodate hundreds of people was, in effect, already approved and as good as granted.

Isaac, in high spirits, returned to England where he drafted a letter of response to those who had applied for membership in his cooperative venture. He hired a secretary, a Miss Christina Mellberg, who corrected the document, made copies then sent out notification to all 2,000 colonists that all was ready. Barr, meanwhile, busied himself scurrying about making arrangements for his flock. Midway through 1902 he notified them in a final letter that all was ready for the great exodus and they should complete their own personal arrangements. In 1903 the entire group set sail for Canada aboard a small, leaking, poorly maintained steamer, the SS *Lake Manitoba*.

The colonists arrived in Halifax, Nova Scotia, on April 12, 1903. The voyage in the twenty-two-year-old ship had been a nightmare which included poor food, intense seasickness, storms for which the Atlantic Ocean is so famous and not nearly enough quarters for such a large group. As a result cabins built for four housed up to eight miserable souls. Midway through the voyage the settlers began to suspect that Isaac Barr was no Moses, was not a good manager, made poor decisions and began to wonder if they had collectively made a great mistake. The grumbling precipitated a near-mutiny against Barr. He managed to diffuse the situation with help from the ship's captain who reminded his passengers that mutiny was punishable by death upon conviction. Barr breathed a sigh of relief unaware that worse lay ahead.

The settlers found on arrival at Halifax, Nova Scotia, that the group was not expected, no shelter had been arranged and no train had been scheduled for furtherance west. As a result there was a delay of many days. The pilgrims were taken in hand by Halifax authorities and put up in sheds on the waterfront to await a train. Local residents aided them with food and clothing.

Barr, in his ignorance of the workings of government, had assumed all would be arranged by the official in Ottawa to whom he had presented his project so many months before. Little did he know that the official had in accordance with rules governing the chain of command merely forwarded the proposal to the next level then forgot about the strange little minister from England with the grandiose scheme. In fact, the project had not yet been considered let alone approved. The realization that nothing had been prepared shook Barr's faith in government, but not in himself.

However, his consternation was nothing compared to the wrath of his colonists who were beginning to see themselves as victims in some sort of grand scam. Only Isaac's glib tongue and obvious sincerity managed to diffuse yet another ugly confrontation. The settlers agreed to give him one more chance to set things straight.

So, while his flock languished in their makeshift quarters, Barr scurried here and there meeting with officials of the federal government and others and making hurried arrangements to move the colonists out of Halifax and on to Saskatchewan.

At last a train was located that could accommodate the large group, and in May the journey resumed. Fortunately the trip across was not too dreadful and Barr began to think all would be well. So did some of the others; but the vast majority decided that a close eye would be kept on their minister.

Eventually they arrived in Saskatoon, itself a small city barely twenty years in existence and still struggling to survive. Barr, having once again failed to look ahead, had not made arrangements for food and accommodation. He could not seem to grasp the importance of arranging details well in advance if one expects to transport many hundreds of people across a wide country in order to drop them off in the middle of a poorly mapped, underpopulated region.

Once again good people came to the rescue and the would-be settlers were put up in barns and sheds, which were drafty and cold. The angry colonists beset Barr with such wrath that he and his faithful secretary fled to the protection of the NWMP office.

The commanding officer in charge assigned a constable to act as a full-time body guard to ensure his safety. Barr found he could travel nowhere without his escort. Everywhere he looked he saw angry colonists; and he had no desire to face them alone. Finally he simply stayed in his meager lodgings, the Mountie outside guarding the entrance. Meantime, the angry crowd milled about plotting Barr's overthrow. Some plotted his demise.

As sometimes happens in cases of extreme provocation providence steps in to control unruly situations. This time providence produced a champion who not only had a sense of management but exercised much influence over his fellow pilgrims. As Barr faltered, this man came forward.

Had it not been for the steadying influence of the Reverend George Exton Lloyd, also an Anglican minister who, fortunately as things transpired, had decided to accompany the pilgrims, Barr would have, sooner or later, been lynched and there were not enough Mounties in the entire territory to save him had the crowd attacked. The colonists, all Britons from the poorer parts of the realm and lacking in social graces, sat plotting in their drafty barns. The scant supply of available food and the incessant prairie dust that swirled around them was driving them all to the end of their limited patience. Had Lloyd not stepped forward when he did there is little doubt the

Reverend Isaac Barr would have been carried to the nearest tree and hanged, armed escort or not. It was just a matter of time.

Lloyd, seeing the gathering storm, quickly took over. He spoke to the crowd managing to soothe them enough that they promised not to do anything right away—at least until he returned. Then he journeyed into Saskatoon, consulted with territory officials, met with representatives of the federal government and eventually set things straight. He then arranged travel from Saskatoon to the land which Barr had actually arranged for the settlers. The original Ottawa bureaucrat had penciled in the area during their preliminary talk and the authorities agreed with Lloyd that the area was not only a good choice but was available under the Homestead Act. Lloyd quickly moved to consolidate the area for the settlers.

Meanwhile, as Lloyd was busy pulling the chestnuts from the fire, a disgraced Isaac Barr, no longer loved by any of the settlers, slunk into Saskatoon with Miss Mellberg and, under cover of darkness, boarded the night train heading south. He fled to Montana.

Barr remained a few years in the United States, married the faithful Christina and eventually fathered two sons. He later moved his family to Australia where he lived until his death in 1937 at the venerable age of ninety.

Isaac Barr to his dying day felt that he had been betrayed by those he had set out to help. He never once admitted the troubles to which he had subjected his settlers were due in the main to his own incompetence, naivete and lack of sound judgement. His failure to investigate situations thoroughly before acting was of no help either.

By the end of 1904, under the leadership of Reverend Lloyd, the majority of the Barr settlers were well established in what proved to be an excellent farming area. Those who chose not to farm established various businesses in the town they built. They named the town Lloydminster to honor the man who had actually saved them. It became, and remains, a prosperous small city. (By a twist of fate when surveyors laid out the boundary line for the new provinces of Saskatchewan and Alberta in 1906, the line ran right down the middle of the town. To this day half the town lies in Alberta; the other half in Saskatchewan. The townspeople, faced with a dilemma, elected to incorporate their town in Alberta. This proved a smart move for the simple reason that taxes in Alberta are less than in Saskatchewan. Isaac would never have thought of that idea.)

There is nothing named to the memory of Isaac Barr.

CHAPTER 11

The West's Most Dangerous Man

JERRY POTTS *Kyi-yo-kosi*
- b. Northwest Territories, 1840
- d. Fort MacLeod, 1896

The rider, his .44 Henry rifle cradled across his knees, sat motionless astride the roan mustang, his gaze fixed on an approaching wagon drawn by two plodding oxen on the trail below. The horseman knew the wagon was laden with hide bags each filled with the deadly potion his people called "firewater," raw alcohol mixed with a number of strange ingredients designed to give color and flavor. They had traded their furs—and ultimately their souls—for this devil's brew; and it was destroying his people more quickly than could any number of wars.

Firewater gained its name through the Natives' practice of testing the liquid before making a purchase. They knew from their trading with the Hudsons' Bay Company that high-proof whiskey burned when touched by a flame. Therefore they insisted the whiskey runners' product do the same. The alcohol used by whiskey runners was always diluted in order to increase volume so they began to lace the stuff with turpentine and black gunpowder. Such a mixture was sure to leap into flame if not explode. To give their brew the reddish color expected of rye whiskey the runners mixed various dyes—and even red ink—to the brew. If the product was red and burned freely, the Indians were satisfied. It is small wonder that firewater was so named. It is equally small wonder that it proved so fatal.

As the rider saw the overall situation, it had come down to a matter of destroying the whisky runners before they destroyed the

Indians. He knew what firewater did because he had once worked for the runners, long ago when he still thought they were legitimate fur traders just as his father had been.

He occasionally wiped a hand across his brow to dispel the beads of sweat caused by the prairie sun beating down hot from the cloudless sky. From time to time errant rivulets of water coursed down the rider's face to disappear into the scrubby stubble of a five-day growth of beard. The water the whiskers failed to arrest dripped to his denim shirt. He was thankful for his broad-brimmed Stetson, once white but now grimy with age and ingrained dust. It shaded his eyes and denied the harsh rays of the sun from tormenting the exposed areas of his craggy, weather-lined face. Each wrinkle bore witness to his many summers in the sun and too many winters of struggle against the winds that blew unfettered and unhindered across the uncluttered prairie flatlands. He looked twenty years older than his thirty-five summers.

The mustang, a tough range pony, did not mind the heat. He had survived his nine years on the unfriendly prairie by adapting to the conditions and exploiting his disposition of sheer cussedness. He had never been more than partly broken, having refused to concede all his rights; but as he had grown older he had learned to tolerate his rider if only because he instinctively knew that should he rebel too often or too violently the rider would either trade him or eat him depending upon his mood of the moment. Besides, he rather liked the strange man who treated him with amiable indifference. The horse and the man, neither more than half-tame, complemented each other in many ways.

The hillock overlooking the trail shielded both horse and rider from the wagon driver's view. They blended so perfectly with the natural dun color of the land even had the wagon driver looked directly at the hillock he would not have seen either. The rider, experienced in the skills of tracking, had positioned his horse to allow only his own head to extend above the crest of the hill. He was an expert in the deadly game he played—this game of seek and kill.

The rider had shadowed the wagon for two days, had trailed it from Fort Benton in what is now the state of Montana to several miles within the Northwest Territory that is now the Canadian province of Saskatchewan. He had, silently and unseen, followed the wagon until it crossed the invisible line the Blackfoot nation called "the Medicine Line" and white men called the border. (The line was so called because to many Natives, the word medicine meant power. On the American side of the border the whites seemed violent and aggressive. On the Canadian side the whites were less violent. Thus, the Americans had aggressive medicine. The Indians knew about the border and thought it the reason for the difference in medicine.) The rider, well aware of the law then in existence, allowed the wagon to pass out of American jurisdiction before he swung his mustang off the trail. The wagon driver was now the under the jurisdiction of British law, a more theory than fact jurisdiction made even more casual by the lack of an established police force. The rider passed the wagon at a distance to move unseen to a point well ahead. He had learned years before that the best way to track such a quarry was to stay well in front and bide time. He had chosen this spot because it offered a good vantage point to a watcher not wishing to be seen.

The wagon, its driver urging the team of sluggish oxen onward, lumbered ever nearer. The animals strained against the traces, their hooves kicking up small dust-devils as they plodded their way along the powder-dry trail.

The wagon drew closer. The rider levered a shell into the rifle's breach. He raised the weapon to his shoulder and leveled the rifle until it pointed directly at the driver. Sighting carefully along the barrel he aligned the front and rear sights, steadied the sight to a point on the driver's chest and squeezed the trigger. The rifle barked, spat a short tongue of flame, belched smoke from seventy grains of black powder as the heavy slug escaped the rifle's muzzle. The rifle kicked upward as the sound rolled and echoed across the barren plain. The mustang, startled by the sudden noise, kicked in a short bucking motion and shied sideways. Then, because the noise was no stranger to his ears, he resumed his interrupted munching.

Through the smoke the rider saw the wagon driver slump forward, turn slightly then slide sideways off the wagon's bench to tumble heavily to the ground below. The wagon passed to reveal him lying motionless on the sunbaked ground. The oxen, the reins gone slack, slowed their pace and stopped. The rider watched a few moments longer before jabbing a booted heel into the mustang's ribs. The horse responded, moved quickly forward, began the descent down the sloping sides of the hillock.

The rider cautiously drew close to the wagon. He quickly determined the whiskey runner was dead, killed instantly when the bullet from the Henry ripped into his chest. Dismounting, he unhitched the oxen from the wagon traces. Thus liberated they wandered slowly away, confused by the sudden freedom. He watched them for a moment. Within a day or two, they would fall prey to some Blackfoot hunting party. The meat would feed a village for a few days.

He then dragged the dead driver back to the wagon where he wrestled the limp weight atop the cargo of whiskey-filled bags. He removed one bag. This he would keep for his own use. Returning his attention to the wagon, he drew a wide-blade skinning knife from his belt, slashed open several bags and watched the potent contents flow out. Reaching into his shirt pocket he retrieved a flat tin, removed a wooden match which he scratched against the wagon, watched it flicker to life then placed it beside the draining liquid. Matches, he mused, were one good thing to have come from the white man. They were much better than using flint to coax a flame from dry grass. Satisfied the match would not go out he turned and walked away.

A pool of alcohol burst into flame with a distinct poof as it ignited and surged to life. The bluish-orange flame quickly increased in volume and intensity. Spreading quickly, the flame caught the liquid soaked bags and wagon wood. Within seconds the entire wagon, cargo and the body of the dead whiskey runner were engulfed in flames. The mustang skittered a few yards distant. He hated fire. All horses do.

The rider retrieved the bag of whiskey he had removed from the wagon, easily overtook the horse, swung into the saddle, jammed the bag between himself and the saddle pommel and, without a backward glance, rode north toward the Cypress Hills. That night he would camp in the familiar hills, cook a rabbit and drink the whiskey. Although he hated the whisky runners, he was much addicted to their product.

The following morning, head pounding and in a foul mood, he rode the remaining few miles to his lodge and a reunion with his two wives. He had been away many weeks. He looked forward to spending some time at home.

A day or two later a hunting party from a village of the Blood Indians, leading two oxen, happened upon the burned-out wagon. They moved their ponies closer, took a long look. They did not dismount for they saw nothing was salvageable. In silence they surveyed the burned wood, the charred wheels, the remains of the hide bags. They scarcely glanced at the charred body, barely recognizable as a man. What had happened on that trail was obvious to them.

"Kyi-yo-kosi," intoned the leader.

The others nodded. They had seen Kyi-yo-kosi's work before.

To the Indians of the Blackfoot nation he was Kyi-yo-kosi, the name given to him the day he was accepted into the Blood tribe as a teenage brave. When he heard it intoned by the shaman his young chest swelled with such pride that even the pain of the initiation rite that had earned him the honor had dulled. Kyi-yo-kosi, Bear Child, was not a name the tribe would have given to just anyone. The name was his because he had proven his bravery. The bear was brother to the Blackfoot nation and he was his child.

To the Blackfoot, the greater nation of which the Blood tribe was a vital segment, he would become known as a hunter of buffalo, a brave warrior, a chief who had gained great victories during several wars between the Blackfoot nation and the Woodland Cree and their allies the Crows. During one such battle his warriors had defeated a much larger force led by the legendary Piapot and the equally famous Crowfoot, both great warrior chiefs. The proof of his prowess were the many scalps hanging from his lodgepole. To the Bloods and their brothers, the Peigans and the Gros Ventres, he was a greatly honored warrior chief. The people of the Crow hated him for many reasons. To the tribes of the Cree nation he was a bitter and vicious enemy whose scalp, though eagerly sought, was never lifted.

White men of peaceful ways knew him as Jerry Potts. To them he was a plainsman, horse trader, guide, interpreter and, to those he liked, a fearless and loyal friend.

To those of evil intent, the whiskey runners and the wolfers (gangs of killers roaming the prairies from 1855 to 1875 who pretended to trade for fur and would then kill the Indian trappers and take their furs), he was the most dangerous man in the west. What made him so ominous to such men is the fact he had once guided the whiskey runners and thus knew the trails they traveled, the campsites they used and the Montana saloons they frequented. Jerry Potts knew these men better than anyone else.

That he was an extremely dangerous man, there was never any

doubt. By the time he was thirty-five he had killed at least that many men, most face to face. He had too much a sense of honor to resort to ambush with the exception of whiskey runners. To those men he would show no honor for they themselves possessed none. A crack shot with rifle and pistol he also knew the ins and outs of knife fighting for it was with his long, wide-blade skinning knife that he had killed his first man at age twenty-two. A drunken braggart named Antoine Primeau challenged him outside a Fort Benton saloon one day, a challenge issued because of some obscure, long-forgotten disagreement.

Primeau entered the contest smug, cocky and confident because Potts was younger and smaller than he. Five minutes later Antoine Primeau lay dying in the dust of Fort Benton's main street. Witnesses said his eyes remained wide in dumbfounded astonishment right up the moment he closed them forever. He had picked on the wrong person at the wrong time.

Jerry Potts was the classic half-breed in that he could never be definitely identified as either white or Native. He had inherited from his Indian mother little of the facial features intrinsic to the Native people of the west—the high cheek bones and coppery complexion were not his—but he was not tall and heavyset as his white father had been.

To the Indians he was sometimes white, sometimes Indian. To white men he appeared more Native than white but he moved freely, not at all uneasily, in white settlements; and in an era where prejudice against those of mixed blood was rampant he numbered many whites among his friends. Several were men of influence.

To the Montana whiskey runners and the wolfers he was anathema for he had named himself their prosecutor, jury, judge and executioner. He was particularly feared by the wolfers, corrupt fur pirates who preyed on Indians. Wolfers had even fewer scruples than those who traded in whiskey. The whiskey merchants at least offered something in trade to obtain furs. Wolfers stole the furs—and killed while doing so.

Potts was to become much admired, respected and depended upon by the NWMP. In the autumn of 1874 he had been hired as trail guide by Inspector Walsh's small force of Mounties. His experience saved the company from certain death. Had he not helped them, they would have perished on the open prairie for they were lost in the uncharted wilderness. The entire troop, there is little doubt, would have died in the cold of the impending winter. Potts admitted years later he helped Walsh and his men mainly because he knew they had come to close the border to the whiskey runners and the wolfers. Had the police come for any other reason, he intimated, he would not have accepted Walsh's offer of work. At the time he was not in need of money having just sold a large herd of horses to Montana ranchers.

His long association with the NWMP began the day he met Walsh in Fort Benton. From that day forward he was their guide, advisor, hunter, mentor and interpreter. He taught the inexperienced lawmen the art of survival against the prairie winters, how to stalk the wily antelope, how to find water where there seemed to be none, how to read the Indian stone markers that showed directions and how to live off the land. He also advised the supply officers on what horses to buy and which ones to refuse. Of course, the horses he recommended were usually from his corral.

Potts was so good at finding the necessary directions that he always knew exactly where he was in that vast sweep of land. On one occasion he was leading Inspector Walsh and a small troop through the Cypress Hills. Reading the stone markers as he went he suddenly stopped his pony. He then rode a short distance one way, turned, rode in yet another direction then another. Walsh caught up to him to enquire mildly, "What's the matter Jerry? Are you lost?"

Potts fixed the inspector with a withering look.

"Nope. Stones wrong," he replied. "Hafta follow grass."

Then, watching for stalks of grass that had been broken and bent by the group that had recently passed that way, he led the troop directly to the camp site they had started for earlier. None of the Mounties had noticed the subtle variations that had been made by the passing travelers through the short prairie grass.

So who was Jerry Potts? How had this Indian brave become white? Or was it the other way around? In fact, it was half of one and half of the other. Both Indians and whites claimed him, and legitimately so.

Jerry Potts was born in a white man's house in a Hudson's Bay trading post in what is now southern Saskatchewan or northern Montana, no one is certain. His father was a Scotsman, Alexander R. Potts, a clerk with the Hudson's Bay Company. His mother, Crooked Back, was a Blood of the Black Elk tribe. Alexander named his son Jerry after his own father and doted on the baby.

Tragically, Alex Potts was murdered by an enraged Indian (nobody knows why, but it was guessed to be a case of mistaken identity) when Jerry was only two years old, barely old enough to know his father. But he must have known him well enough to vow vengeance, for fifteen years later he hunted the killer, found him in an Indian village near the town of Kalispell in northwestern Montana, shot him and took his scalp.

Crooked Back grieved for her husband until she met a white trapper, the notorious Alexander Harvey. (He was known for being a great drinker and a deadly rifle shot and possessing a terrible temper that got him into various troubles.) He took her as his wife and accepted three-year-old Jerry as part of the relationship. Harvey fathered Crooked Back's second son, whom she named No Chief.

Shortly after, in 1844, Harvey moved them to Fort MacKenzie, in what is now South Dakota on the Missouri River, when he was named that post's manager by the American Fur Trading Company. What Jerry thought of his new brother is unknown but he liked his new father. Harvey also took a great liking to Jerry and proudly introduced him to colleagues as "my son."

Harvey, who figures prominently in the checkered history of the American Fur Trading Company, was a psychotic killer (known for his "shoot first, ask questions later" attitude, particularly when dealing with employees) but he treated Crooked Back and her children kindly. He taught Jerry, still only four years of age, how to ride a mustang colt he had acquired for him, how to get along with whites on even terms, how to recognize friendly whites and those not friendly. He also instilled in the little boy his philosophy that only the strong survive. It was this philosophy that sustained Jerry Potts throughout his life.

Harvey had been with his "family" about three years when he had a serious run-in with his employers. The owners of The American Fur Company were growing alarmed at his habit of killing anyone—including customers and employees—who disagreed with him. The situation came to a boil when Harvey shot and killed a trapper he thought had stolen one of the company's pigs. The company might not have raised much objection under normal circumstances but Harvey's victim had been the company's best supplier of marten pelts. The loss of such a supplier meant great losses in future pelts. The prospect of such a loss in profits overrode the company's loyalty to a post manager. Harvey was severely reprimanded, the penalty being a sharp cut in pay.

Enraged at what he considered shabby treatment he quit and announced plans to start his own company. He deserted Jerry, No Chief and Crooked Back without so much as a formal goodbye. The reason of course was that he was returning to St. Louis and an Indian wife and her two children would neither endear him to that city's society nor enhance his chances of finding monetary supporters for his new company. He returned to the city where he began his quest to find backers. Then, within a few weeks of his arrival, he fell ill with a severe viral infection and died within a day or two. Alexander Harvey, one of the west's more notorious figures, was dead at age forty-five.

Jerry, fatherless once again, would likely have become just another nondescript kid roaming from village to village along the western banks of the Missouri River had his mother not returned north to her own people. She stayed with her father until the day she met another Scotsman, Andrew Dawson.

Dawson, a kindly man who held a good position with the Hudson's Bay Company, took a great liking to Crooked Back. Within hours of that first meeting he asked her father to allow Crooked Back to move in with him. Dawson offered a fine gift of horses and a new rifle which were accepted. Crooked Back and her sons departed her father's lodge for that of Andrew Dawson. Once again Jerry Potts, now five years old, found himself living in a wooden house inside an HBC fort.

The union remained happy for several years. Dawson taught Jerry and No Chief how to speak "proper English." No Chief proved to be an unwilling student, quite the opposite of Jerry, so Dawson concentrated his attention to the more teachable boy. While Dawson taught the two boys to speak English, for some reason he never taught them to read or write. This oversight is notable because he taught Jerry the conventions of his own lower-middle class Scottish society. Under Dawson's tutelage young Jerry became a white man.

Jerry called Dawson "father" for at least five years and would have been happy to stay with him had Crooked Back not begun to once again pine for her own people. Dawson was too kindly a man to refuse her that choice, so she, No Chief and Jerry returned once again to the village of the Black Elk tribe.

Jerry Potts, now aged eleven or twelve, immediately took to the

Indian way of life. Under the masterful hands of successful braves he was taught to hunt with and without weapons, how to use the Henry rifle that was the firearm of choice at the time, how to use a bow and arrow with deadly accuracy, how to ride half-broken mustangs without benefit of saddle. As eager a student of his Indian tutors as he had been under Harvey and Dawson, Potts quickly mastered the Indian method of riding at a full gallop while firing his rifle, pistol or bow with deadly accuracy while hanging precariously from either side of his horse. While he never used a saddle when he rode with his own people, he usually did when riding with whites. This trait seemed to determine which culture he was embracing at the time.

By his fifteenth year Potts had passed all the traditional rites of passage including the final agony of the sun dance ritual. The sun dance was the last rite required of the fledgling brave before acceptance into the ranks of warriors. It was a painful, debilitating ritual that left the would-be warrior weakened and often delirious. Many took weeks to recover completely. There were many who did not complete it, often because they died during the ordeal.

The initiate prepared himself for the sun dance through an initial phase of dancing, fasting and meditation. For the second and final phase the shamans, using sharpened needles fashioned from buffalo bones, threaded long rawhide thongs through and under his chest muscles. The initiate was then tied to a tree or secure pole by the thongs and left alone to free himself at whichever moment he chose. The achievement of successful passage from boyhood to warrior meant the youth required a violent motion to free himself from the thongs. There was only one way to do it for the thongs were tied in such a manner they could not be loosened or cut and slipped out.

Freedom could be achieved only by tearing the thongs from his chest muscles directly through the flesh at the bottom of the muscles. The fledgling brave had the choice of doing so immediately or to remain tied to the pole in a state of absolute silence for up to three days before freeing himself. Potts, perhaps feeling he had to prove something because of his mixed-blood status, chose to remain the full three days. His ordeal, and the manner in which he handled it, assured him a place among the warriors. It also marked him as a future chief.

After the painful wounds had healed, he was taken for the first time on a hunt as a hunter not a learner. Although the great herds of buffalo had long vanished, many small herds still roamed the plains. There were adequate numbers to satisfy the needs of small villages and enough that the hunters could practice old traditions of riding down the mighty beasts on horseback. Jerry Potts, now called Kyi-yo-kosi, reveled in the thrill of the hunt, the tracking, the chase and the kill. Great was his pride when he returned with his group from his first hunt, horses and men laden with huge pieces of buffalo meat.

Kyi-yo-kosi presented to Crooked Back the hides of the shaggy beasts he had personally brought down. She worked diligently over many days to scrape, cure, tan and dry the hides until they were bleached almost white. She sewed them together with rawhide thongs stitched tightly to ensure strength.

When the hides were ready, the proud young warrior made paints from buffalo grease mixed with powders from crushed stones and juices of various berries. He decorated his hides with circles, pictures of buffalo and horses and the symbols of his tribe in a manner befitting a hunter. Then he secured them tightly over and around long poles that reached toward the sky. When the tepee was complete he, his brother and Crooked Back moved into his new lodge. It would be home for quite some time.

By the time he reached his twentieth birthday Potts, now known exclusively as Kyi-yo-kosi, had been accepted into several of the secret warrior societies which prevailed in large numbers throughout the Blackfoot nation. During these years he led raiding parties against the Blackfoots' traditional enemies, the Crow and the Cree. He counted many coups, collected many scalps, suffered wounds and earned the respect of friends and enemies alike. (To "count coup" the warrior had to stand over his downed foe and touch him with his lance. This was sometimes dangerous because the foe was not always dead and might have enough life left in him for one final attack.) In recognition of his bravery in battle, his unquestioned leadership abilities and his knowledge of the prairies, he was named a minor chief of the Blackfoot nation when he was about twenty-five. Had history moved in a different direction, he would likely have become a great war chief.

History, however, was not favoring the Indians. White men in great numbers had already begun to move into the territory, especially south of the Medicine Line. Some plowed the flatlands for farming, others acquired herds of cattle and horses while others built homesteads. A great number dug large holes into the sides of mountains and took out shiny metal. The whites first killed the buffalo then they forced the Natives onto reservations. The days of the nomadic Indians and the hunters were rapidly drawing to a close.

The year was about 1868 when some great chiefs of the Blackfoot and Cree, seeing that intertribal wars were diminishing the numbers of their people, entered into a pact that saw the end of the great wars. The pact for the most part held quite well. From that year fighting became limited to skirmishes between scattered bands. It meant the day of the warrior was also drawing to a close.

Kyi-yo-kosi saw this and knew he, too, must move in a different direction. He once again donned his persona of Jerry Potts and again embraced, at least to some extent, the ways of the white man. He did not leave his prairie lodges (he was now living in northwest Montana), preferring to live as an Indian, but he began to move more and more in the white society he had not quite forgotten. In the transition he became a business man.

About 1867 he began to build a small herd of good range ponies, all sturdy mustangs. Potts was resourceful, had an eye for horse flesh and became one of the shrewdest horse-traders of the era. By the time he was thirty, in 1870, he had become a moderately wealthy man through trading. The going rate for a good horse was at the time at least $75, so his large inventory showed his wealth. He carefully worked his small herd into a large one that was never to number less than 100 first-rate mustangs. Once and sometimes twice each year he would cut out several dozens and herd them to Fort Benton. There he would trade and sell during the day. At night he would drink and fight.

After a couple of weeks of hard dealing and harder drinking he would pocket his cash, round up the horses he had taken in trade and travel north to begin again the work that was needed to increase his herd. During those years, when a man's wealth was measured by the number of horses he owned, Jerry Potts was wealthy indeed, perhaps the second wealthiest man in the territory. His habit of carrying large amounts of cash during these business trips was well known. When he journeyed to Fort Benton to buy horses, he would carry as much as $1,000 with which to make the transactions. People knew he carried such amounts but they also knew he was Jerry Potts, so he was left alone.

If some of his horses carried a number of diverse brands it

meant nothing. Potts could produce bills of sale for most of them even if he could not read them himself. Those without papers, if they were American horses, were sold in Canada while paperless Canadian horses ended up in the south. Those branded with the markings of the U.S. Cavalry were sold as far north as possible unless he had papers proving they had been purchased at a U.S. Army auction.

Following a sale he would exchange cash for a receipt written by someone else. On the paper he then penciled a rough symbol, a mark known far and wide as his, and the deal was done.

In 1869 Jerry Potts took ongoing employment as a guide for groups of whiskey runners. He guided their wagons from Fort Benton to Fort Whoop-Up and other forts that had been established by whiskey runners throughout what is now southern Alberta. The trails were long, fraught with danger and poorly marked. He liked the money for it allowed him to buy horses and he got along with his employers because he knew how to deal with them. On occasion a driver would rebel, take exception to being told what to do by a half-breed or imply that Potts was not humble enough in his presence. He would soon discover that Potts had no intention of being humble in front of anyone.

Potts never said much to such a man. He gave him four choices: leave the guiding to Potts, go on alone, turn back to Fort Benton or reach for his pistol. The first choice was the wisest. He had no hesitation in obliging the man who decided on the fourth, the foolish, choice. Those who fell to his pistol, and there were several, were left at the side of the trail. If a companion wished to bury the unfortunate fellow that was all right with Potts. He would wait patiently as the grave mound was completed.

"Why bother?" he would ask. "Coyotes will only dig him up."

It was during his early years that Potts had his first tastes of the whiskey that was called firewater and it addicted him to alcohol. It was an dependence he was never to overcome and it eventually killed him—that and the strong black cigarillos he smoked. He guided the runners for quite some time before he saw what firewater was doing to his people, but he seems not to have minded. Then, two events turned him against his employers and against the sale of alcohol to Indians. Unfortunately, it did not turn him against whiskey for his own use.

In 1870 Potts was thirty and still guiding the whiskey runners from village to village and fort to fort, when his mother and No Chief were murdered by a Gros Ventre brave named Good Young Man. The circumstances leading to the murders were tragic and a direct result of firewater.

The entire population of a Blood village had journeyed to Fort Kipp, located in southwest Alberta just north of Fort Whoop-Up. There they camped in sight of the walls alongside several other tribes. All had come intent on trading. Shortly after sunrise the men from Fort Kipp came to the Indians' camp with many gallons of firewater. This they exchanged for everything of value the Indians had to offer. Then, leaving the Indians with the alcohol, the traders returned to the fort and barred the gates. They knew what was going to happen.

Three large camps of Indians, none of which were particularly friendly with the others, began to drink. At first, the celebrations were happy with singing, dancing and friendly wrestling and other competitions; but by noon the fun had taken a violent twist. Arguments broke out among many of the younger men. Soon the situation was out of hand. By midafternoon nearly everyone in the village was drunk. Fights were breaking out with injuries occurring as a result. The three chiefs tried to restore order but they were all too old to physically control the fighters and their words fell on deaf ears.

Crooked Back and No Chief had come to the Blood camp to visit a relative that day. However, both joined the celebrations. No Chief took an active part in the games. Crooked Back, although soon enough drunk, became alarmed at what she was seeing and wanted to leave but No Chief refused. He then went over to the camp of a group from the Gros Ventre tribe where he joined in their merriment. (White trappers gave this tribe the name Gros Ventre, which in French means big belly. The Indians called themselves Atsina, which means the people.)

As the day wore toward evening Good Young Man began to argue with No Chief. The two began to shove each other. Suddenly a knife flashed. In a fit of rage Good Young Man stabbed No Chief who fell to the ground. Other Gros Ventres moved in to attack No Chief who immediately drew his pistols and began firing wildly. When the fracas ended No Chief lay dead, murdered by Good Young Man. Several Gros Ventres, dead or seriously wounded, lay on the ground. No Chief had managed to kill two of his attackers

119

and wound several others but he and his twelve bullets were no match for an angry mob numbering in the dozens.

In an act of sheer contempt Good Young Man, who had escaped injury, dragged No Chief's body to the edge of the camp. He left it there for the camp dogs to gnaw on. Anguished, mother ran to son. Crooked Back chased off the snarling dogs despite being bitten badly. Sitting beside her dead son she cradled his bloody head in her arms and began to wail the death song of the Blood people.

Good Young Man, hearing the death wail, shouted at her to shut up. Crooked Back continued the wail. In his drunken rage Good Young Man turned on Crooked Back, clubbed her into unconsciousness then allowed the dogs to resume their grisly feasting. Crooked Back died in agony beside her son, killed by the snarling pack of dogs, while a large crowd taunted her.

Jerry Potts heard of the murders weeks later. His thoughts when he heard are not known. Such fights were not new to him and it is likely he would have dismissed No Chief's death as misadventure had it occurred as simply the result of a drunken brawl. Even Crooked Back's death might have been forgiven had it been the direct result of the binge. After all, Crooked Back had willingly jóined the party. Potts knew what was happening to his people, how the deadly firewater had already wreaked great havoc, how it had turned brother against brother, tribe against tribe and how it was destroying a once-proud people.

No, the deaths of his brother and mother would not have upset Jerry Potts had that been all it was for Jerry Potts did not possess compassion; he had seen too much cruelty in his thirty years to be highly affected by two deaths during a brawl. What made the difference in his thinking was the indignity of Good Young Man's contemptuous treatment of the dead. His deliberate outrage against the dead No Chief and the grieving Crooked Back when he let them be eaten by dogs was not forgivable. By his actions Good Young Man assured his own death. Potts could never forgive him.

Tradition demanded Jerry Potts avenge those two senseless murders. It was a law he respected for he had taken vengeance upon his father's killer despite the fact that he was not yet two at the time his father died. He was an adherent of Indian law and that law called for vengeance against anyone who killed a family member in a dishonorable manner.

But much of his upbringing had also made him aware of the

white man's law so he may have felt a twinge of indecision as to which way he should turn. If he did, he was not long bothered by it. To seek justice under the law of the white man would have been a useless undertaking. White man's courts, even where established, had no time for dealing with an Indian who killed other Indians and there was as yet no law in the northern territories save that of the Indian.

Potts therefore interpreted the situation as did most of those who were developing the land at the time. He must seek the justice dispensed by the west's three most reliable judges—Winchester, Sharps and Henry. Potts, who was not without a keen sense of humor, often said the only jury he would ever trust was the one that served Judge Colt. He meant, of course, the six bullets in his revolver.

When Potts heard about the murders of his mother and brother he seems also to have suddenly realized that whiskey, not the encroaching white men, was the Indians' real enemy. He placed no more blame for the murders on Good Young Man than he placed on those who had sold the firewater to the Indians camped that day outside Fort Kipp. From that moment on not a whiskey runner was safe from his deadly rifle. Potts quietly declared war upon his erstwhile companions.

It was more than a year before Potts caught up with Good Young Man. He tracked him throughout the northern reaches of Alberta's foothills, possibly as far as the Rocky Mountains, then south to the Missouri River and north again into southern Saskatchewan. It proved a difficult trail until one day he saw his quarry, with a companion, at a distance but riding toward him. He unsheathed his Henry, levered a shell into the breach, swung his horse into full gallop and rode directly for Good Young Man. When Good Young Man saw Potts it was too late. Knowing the danger he was in Good Young Man turned to flee.

The chase was short. Potts disposed of Good Young Man with one shot. Good Young Man slid from his horse to hit the ground where he lay, dying in agony, with Potts' rifle bullet imbedded in his liver. Potts motioned to Good Young Man's companion, a youth called Morning Writing, to leave. He would spare him because Morning Writing had never harmed Potts. There was that certain fairness about him. Besides, a witness was handy in spreading the word that a man had settled the score. If a man was to be feared people had to know about him. As Morning Writing spurred his horse in escape Potts dismounted and strode purposefully to where Good Young Man lay.

Potts looked down at the dying man, unsheathed his skinning knife and quickly scalped Good Young Man. To Potts mind it was fitting that the man was still alive as that was the final retribution for the crime he had committed against Crooked Back and No Chief. Potts took the Indian's guns and horse as payment for the wrong he had done to Potts. Under Indian law it was payment rendered. He watched until Good Young Man breathed his last then, remounting his horse, Potts lead the latest addition to his herd as he rode toward home.

During the years between 1870 and 1876 Potts also hired out as guide to various parties of men who were invading the Black Hills of the Dakotas in search of gold. He had no qualms about this because the Black Hills were Sioux lands—and Potts had no love for the Sioux. He was in great demand because he always brought his employers safely back from their excursions, although they often had to fight their way there and back. During those years Potts took many scalps from the heads of Sioux warriors who attacked his groups.

Potts would not have guided such men had they wished to go into the Montana or Alberta hill country to mine the lands of the Blackfoot. Perhaps he felt the gold seekers would be content to stay in the Black Hills and not venture westward into Blackfoot country.

Throughout his life Potts remained in great demand as a guide because he knew every trail from Fort Edmonton to the southern lands of the Cheyenne and all the lands between those trails. He could find game when all others had returned to camp empty-handed. During these years he apportioned his white identity with his Indian persona.

Though Potts had been born a Blood, he became a member of the Peigan tribe when he married two sisters, Panther Woman and Spotted Killer. Under Indian law a man became a member of the tribe into which he married. Between his two wives he sired several sons and daughters. He eventually came to consider himself a Peigan (which his continuing family regards him to this day) but he kept the name, Kyi-yo-kosi, given him by the Bloods. How much of him the women actually saw is debatable as he was away much of the time, particularly after he had taken on the task of guiding the police force around the vast territory. He also spent much time on business trading and selling his horses. His trading route extended from Fort Edmonton to southern Montana, east to the Dakotas and west to what is now Idaho.

While Potts abhorred whiskey runners, he had no such hatred for the product as it applied to him. He was no stranger to firewater. He preferred Hudson Bay whiskey and rum when he could get it but would settle for beer, Jamaican ginger, extract of vanilla, a patent medicine called Perry Davis' Painkiller and, if nothing else was available, red ink. When drunk he could be troublesome. His drunken exploits would fill several books.

One night in Fort Benton he and a friend, identified only as Steele, took to arguing about which of them was the better marksman. They decided the best way to settle the matter was to engage in a contest. The loser would have to buy the drinks for the rest of the week. They decided the ideal way to run the contest was to take turns and see who could "trim the mustache" of the other. This little game determined who could put a bullet closest to the opponent's head without actually hitting him.

Each man went to opposite ends of the saloon, a distance of perhaps sixty feet. Each took his place with his back to the wall. The normal hubbub of the crowded room hushed. A referee, chosen from the onlookers tossed a coin. Potts called, won the toss then elected to fire first. The referee hollered to the bystanders to press against the far wall well out of range. Everyone complied. They all knew full well how errant bullets could be when fired from pistols—especially pistols in the hands of two drunks. Side bets were hastily made with Potts the favorite to win. The referee then turned his attention to the two duelists and nodded. Potts raised his pistol, aimed and fired. The bullet holed its way into the wall less than a half inch from Steele's beard. Then it was Steele's turn. He, too, smashed his shot into the wall very close to Potts' chin.

"Nothin' proved," yelled the referee. "Both shots too close to determine anythin'."

"We'll do it again," Potts decided.

"No good," said Steele. "We gotta shoot at the same time."

"Sure," said Potts.

At that moment Sherrif Joe Kipp, the law in Fort Benton, entered the saloon. He had come to investigate the two shots. (He himself was probably never a whiskey trader but he tolerated the lawless element and was elected year after year.)

"What are you two up to?" he demanded.

The situation was explained as Kipp listened attentively.

"Now ain't that just Jim-dandy," he said at last, "the entire territory will be happy to learn which of you two bozos is the best shot. But if you keep this up you'll probably just kill each other. Then who'll collect the week's free whiskey? And who'll pay for it?"

"Umm," replied Potts. "Joe speaks truth."

Steele and Potts holstered their guns and strolled back to the bar to continue their argument in peaceful discussion. Joe Kipp stayed long enough to see if the two would behave. This wasn't the first time he had been called out to settle such disputes. Only the week before two wolfers had tried to settle an argument by shooting glasses off each other's heads. At the first shot one died with a bullet between his eyes while his friends lamented, not his death, but that the man had been holding a glass filled with whiskey and "...the clumsy fool spilled the whiskey on the floor." Kipp wondered how in the world he had allowed himself to be talked into running for sheriff. Guys like Jerry Potts, he decided, would likely be his downfall.

Although Potts was unable to read or write he was able to recognize his name in the newspaper whenever someone pointed it out. They often did for he was frequently mentioned in news items printed in the Helena *Herald* and other Montana newspapers. He would have someone read him the article then nod in agreement or scowl in disapproval.

Illiterate though he may have been, he could speak many languages. He was fluent, if laconic, in English. He spoke all the various Blackfoot dialects and was fluent in Crow and Assiniboine. He had a better than average ability in Cree (which he would speak only when necessary). He was passable in several Sioux dialects and knew just enough French to get along with the Metis when it suited his purpose.

Despite the tutelage of his third father, he never really understood Andrew Dawson's preoccupation with what the man had called "social graces." He could never understand, for instance, why white settlers equipped their houses with chamber pots. "Why," he once asked a Mountie, "would anyone piss in a good cooking bowl when he has the entire prairie at his feet?"

Potts kept his Indian totems active all his life for he was highly superstitious. He wore his magic talisman—a cat skin—under his shirt at all times and tied all his captured scalps to the lodgepole of his main tepee. Still, he wore the clothing of the white man most of the time including a Stetson hat that sported a wide headband. His bushy, drooping mustache was as stylish as that of any white man.

From a distance the stocky, bowlegged Potts looked like a white trapper in his buckskin clothing, his hat at a jaunty angle upon his head. The two pistols hanging from his gun belt complemented the heavy caliber rifle which never left his side. He owned several rifles, including a Winchester .44-75, but he preferred the Henry. Under his jacket he kept at least two small-bore pistols. On his leg was strapped a long-blade skinning knife. He always kept a small pistol inside a hideaway pocket, a practice that saved his life on several occasions.

By the time he was thirty-five he had killed many men, most of whom had been whiskey runners and wolfers, a few Indians who had crossed him plus several others who had either harmed the Indian population in general or his own family members in particular. There is no way of knowing just how many Crows, Crees and Sioux fell before his rifles in battle. The number of scalps that adorned his lodgepole has been estimated from ninety to well over one hundred, all but a few taken in battle.

Potts' unquenchable thirst for alcohol was legendary. On one occasion Inspector MacLeod, having arrested a whiskey runner on the trail, told Potts to take the runner, wagon and whiskey to Fort Macleod and have him placed in jail pending MacLeod's return. By the time Potts and his prisoner reached Fort MacLeod, however, all the whiskey was gone. The two had developed a thirst on the dusty trail and consumed the alcohol to the last drop while on the trail. The two arrived at Fort MacLeod in such a happy state the prisoner had not even tried to escape. However, without the evidence there was no case so the runner was freed. However, the warning never to return was serious and the man was not seen again.

Potts' employment with the NWMP did not end his personal vendetta against the rum runners—even after they had been effectively run out of business. When a cousin was murdered by a whiskey trader in Montana, Potts hunted the man down. He encountered him on the main street of Fort Benton, called a challenge and killed him in a face-to-face shootout. The man died from a single bullet that struck him directly in the right eye.

However, from September, 1874, when he was hired as a guide

by Inspector French his vendetta against the runners diminished. The police were in control and the Canadian side of the medicine line had become peaceful. He moved his lodges into Canada but still ventured into Montana, mostly on business and he still engaged in a few gunfights there but his days in Canada became peaceful.

His association with the "redcoats," as he called them, was to last twenty-two years. He was never paid less than ninety dollars per month for his services, a much higher wage than other guides, and three times a police constable's salary. Even city marshals in large cities such as Abilene or Dodge City often earned less than that amount.

Potts' long partnership with the new force that was then just beginning to police the Territories worked exceedingly well. With the expulsion of the whiskey runners and the wolfers, Potts settled down to confine his activities to serving as guide and interpreter as well as horse trading. He ceased working at age fifty-eight only because the pain of throat and lung cancer so wracked his body that he could no longer ride.

Potts as a guide had no equal. As an interpreter he fell short at times, not in the translation but in the brevity thereof. Although he spoke all the Indian languages of the prairies, he could never see the point of reciting word for word the speeches of the chiefs.

"Chiefs talk too much," he always said. "Talk much; say nothing."

His weakness in interpretation lay in his habit of relaying the speaker's message in the fewest words possible. At meetings between government officials and chiefs he would listen intently then, following each speech, would condense what had been said into as few short sentences as possible.

Once, a Blackfoot chief, renowned for eloquence, made an extremely long, flowery, impassioned speech to a delegation of visiting officials who had arrived from Ottawa to sign an historic treaty. When the chief finally ceased speaking Potts remained silent as if fully digesting the colorful language. Finally, the Ottawa delegates grew impatient. One asked Potts what the chief had said.

"Oh," the laconic Potts replied with a shrug, "he says he's damned glad you're here."

"Surely he said more than that," the official replied.

"Yeah. He says he'll sign the treaty," Potts answered as he walked off in search of a drink.

On another occasion Inspector MacLeod asked what lay beyond a high rising hill ahead, hoping no doubt that Potts would tell him there was fresh water, good grass for the horses and a comfortable site to set up camp for the night.

Potts muttered, "Just 'nuther damn hill."

Always superstitious about omens, Potts prophesied his impending death a few months before he rode out on what would be his final patrol. He had discovered that a small-caliber bullet, which for more than thirty years had been imbedded in a muscle near his neck, had mysteriously disappeared. To his mind, the strange disappearance meant he had lost a talisman that had long brought him luck. (Apparently, at a barracks party a constable removed the bullet by making a small incision with a pen knife. Upon sobering up the distraught Potts told his friends he would surely die within weeks.) He set about putting his affairs in order, telling his sons who was to receive this horse or that rifle in what he considered a fair and equitable division of his goods and chattels.

When he died he was laid to rest with the full honors of the NWMP. The funeral was attended by NWMP personnel with whom he had worked, including many who traveled long distances to attend, and by many dozens of Indians from the Fort MacLeod area. There was also a small contingent of whites from Montana. The funeral was followed by a three-volley rifle salute, a fitting service for a warrior chief.

The *MacLeod Gazette* eulogized him in glowing terms. "Jerry Potts is dead," it began. Then it went on to list his achievements. The editor lamented that this "truly remarkable frontiersman" had never been given the recognition that had been showered upon the likes of Davy Crockett, Jim Bridger and many others whose exploits paled in comparison with those of Potts. In retrospect, one can only agree.

Yet his name lives on, not only in Canada's history books, but in the real-life exploits of some of his grandchildren. Three of his descendants become police officers in the RCMP. A great-granddaughter, Janet Potts, became one of the first women to join the force. Fittingly, she was the first aboriginal woman to enter the service. Her graduation parade at Regina was held not quite one hundred years from the date that Jerry Potts met Inspector Walsh and in so doing rescued the first members of the NWMP.

CHAPTER 12

The Traveling Firewater Salesman

ANTOINE LUCANAGE
- b. Quebec, 1830
- d. Vancouver Island, B.C., 1865

Antoine Lucanage came to British Columbia with one thing on his
mind: he was going to become king of the whiskey dealers then
retire to Quebec with a fortune. Instead he became a hunted man
with a large bounty on his head and met a brutal death in an isolated cove on the rugged northeast shore of Vancouver Island.

Lucanage is truly a man of mystery. It is well established that he
was brutal, even fiendish—a man quick on the trigger and more than
capable with a knife. He was a back-shooter who probably never
faced down anyone in his life. Certainly he was not the type to
engage in a fair gunfight. Instead he would bide his time then
ambush his tormentor. The total number of men he killed, besides a
B.C. police officer, is not known.

Had it not been for the months of his life spent in B.C., it is
unlikely that Antoine Lucanage would be known to have actually
existed. Court records from Victoria determine his name, his age
and his place of birth and little else. Had he remained in his native
Quebec he would likely have remained an anonymous entity
because neither Quebec police records nor the provincial archives
disclose any knowledge of the fellow. It can be surmised he spent
his first thirty years here and there in and around Quebec leading
what might be described as an uneventful life. Nowhere does his
name appear as being involved either in criminal activity, which in
the quaint phraseology of Canadian authorities would have had him

listed as being "...known to police..." or in any other type of activity. On the other hand, he may well have been active in such places as Maine or New Hampshire as French Canadian trappers and woodsmen moved freely across the poorly guarded border.

Lucanage, for whatever reasons, decided Quebec held nothing for him (perhaps he was wanted or being watched) and decided to flee. Whatever happened he headed west sometime prior to 1860 for it was during that year he showed up in Victoria. How long it took him to make the journey, how long he tarried here and there along the way or whether he worked, hunted, trapped, robbed or went directly is unknown. It is likewise unknown if he began his new life in Victoria engaged in gainful employment prior to setting himself up in the whiskey trade. If that was the case, and it is unlikely, he obviously did not take to the work-a-day world for he soon went into the business of selling firewater whiskey to Indians, a serious offense in the eyes of the law.

Lucanage, however, had devised a master plan. He had seen how the Victoria police, despite being understaffed most of the time, really had a very impressive arrest record, and discouraged the men who dealt alcohol in the shadowy byways of the streets along the waterfront. Lucanage deemed himself smarter than the others for he decided the only way to avoid capture was to stay well clear of areas populated by whites, especially those places with police forces.

The plan he devised was novel. He decided to operate from an island hideaway on the northern coast where he could mix cheap grain alcohol into the evil firewater. After everything was mixed, it became a fiery liquor that resembled rye whiskey in everything but purity.

He began his enterprise sometime during 1861 or early 1862. Obtaining a sailboat he loaded it to its limits with five-gallon cans of grain alcohol, cheap but lethal, as well as the other items necessary in the production of firewater, things like black gunpowder and red dye. Then he sailed northward until he found a suitable island. There he built a small camp on his never identified island, mixed his brew, refilled the cans, reloaded his sturdy sailboat and began making house calls.

Natives along the coast had developed a hankering for firewater and, just as he had reasoned, were pleased to deal in the convenience of their own villages. They traded furs and other valuables, even cash when they had some.

Business proved very brisk as Lucanage made his way from village to village. Sometimes he was run off by chiefs who were well aware of the evils of alcohol, but in many villages he was welcomed. When his supply ran out he had only to sail to any reasonably sized settlement along the coast where he could sell his furs and replenish his alcohol. Grain alcohol could be purchased in five gallon cans at an average cost of one dollar each at local drug and general stores. While there was no limit on the number of cans that could be purchased, he had to be careful not to raise the suspicions of the town's lawman as a large purchase of alcohol was a sure-fire tip that the purchaser was a whiskey runner. That problem was solved by dealing at settlements that had no permanent police presence, which included just about every settlement along the coast. Once his boat was loaded, he would sail northward once again.

Lucanage was very wary as he made his rounds, although he was quite aware his endeavor was reasonably secure. B.C. had so few lawmen to police the vast area in which he traveled he knew the chances of being caught were slim. Missionaries, shamans and chiefs as well as concerned civilians had no use for whiskey runners and wanted them out of business but few ever saw such men actively engaging in their trade. Those addicted to the fiery brew were not about to endanger a dependable source of the illicit poison; those who did not want the runners around were reluctant to make a long, sometimes dangerous, trip all the way to a police post to complain. These factors allowed Lucanage to ply his evil trade as long as he did.

Because of the territory he covered, it is thought that from time to time he took in partners and may have headed a gang of whiskey runners known to be working the coastal waters. But he likely worked by himself for the most part.

Despite the shortage of lawmen, the apathy of many natives, distance and the size of the area Lucanage had at his disposal he was eventually reported and soon identified. A wanted poster was issued for his apprehension. Realizing he was being hunted he became even more cautious in his dealings. Always elusive, Lucanage now became almost invisible.

However, as it always does for bad men, time eventually ran out on Antoine Lucanage. His final days began the day he ambushed and killed Constable John D. B. "Jack" Ogilvie (b.1830) aboard the coastal ship *Langley* on May 6, 1865. Ogilvie became the first of several B.C. Police Force officers to be killed in B.C. during the days of the Canadian wild west.

From January to April, 1865, Lucanage had been peddling his wares along the mainland's coast between Cape Caution and the Skeena River. Perhaps his long months of success had filled him with the sense of overconfidence and immortality the ancient Greeks had called *hubris*. His next move points to that strange madness.

By the end of April the merchant prince had run out of alcohol and, despite the fact that he knew wanted posters naming him were displayed in every sizeable town, he boldly sailed his boat right into Bella Coola, a medium-sized town, which at the time was located on Campbell Island near Queen's Sound. His intention was to stay a day or two enjoying the civilization the settlement offered, purchase replacement alcohol from the local pharmacy and general store then depart for his island.

He managed to carry out part of his plan when he sold his bundles of prime furs, checked into a local hotel where he placed a large amount of cash in the hotel safe for secure keeping then stashed his gear in the room assigned. He decided to visit the saloon for a drink. He was about half way to the saloon when he was seen by the area's only lawman, Constable Ogilvie, who recognized Lucanage from a wanted poster.

Ogilvie, on a routine patrol, had come to Bella Coola only the day before intending to stay a day or two, write a procedures report then depart on the next leg of his seemingly endless patrol. He had reported in at the small government post to use the facilities there to compose his reports. The small building was used by whatever government agents happened to be in town at the moment. It also held the town's jail, actually a tiny cell in the corner of a back room. Usually it was empty because Bella Coola had no permanently established law officer. Minor fracases were handled by the townspeople, but in cases of serious nature local citizens would apprehend the culprit if possible and keep him securely under wraps until the police could arrive.

Ogilvie finished his reports then stepped out into the street for the short walk to a cafe and a bite to eat. As he walked he suddenly realized he was looking directly at a man whose description matched a wanted poster he had just looked at. He stopped for a better look, to make sure this was indeed the right man. Lucanage, who was facing another direction, had not seen the lawman. Ogilvie, well aware the poster noted Lucanage should be considered dangerous, drew his pistol and walked quietly up to him.

"Antoine Lucanage," the lawman said quietly, "you are under arrest. Reach high in the air then turn slowly around."

Lucanage, stunned, started to walk away but, hearing the ominous click of a pistol being hammered back, quickly changed his mind. He thrust his arms straight up and did as he was told. He was quickly frisked, placed in handcuffs and hustled off to the town's jail.

With the fugitive safely ensconced in the tiny cell Ogilvie sought out the captain of a schooner scheduled for departure the following morning—destination New Westminster. He gave the captain the necessary papers to be presented to police when the ship docked in New Westminster and assured the skipper they would be pleased to take the fugitive off his hands. They would also pay him the usual fee for such service. The captain agreed to take the prisoner. A few minutes before the ship was due to sail, Lucanage was hustled aboard in chains and secured in the ship's brig.

"Lock up this fellow securely," Ogilvie told the captain. "He is extremely dangerous and very cunning."

"My brig is secure," the captain assured the officer. "He would have to be more than cunning to escape it."

Antoine Lucanage, however, was not only cunning he had certain skills. One of those skills was the ability to slip out of locks and shackles. (Lucanage's hands were small and his wrists were big. Such features mad it easy to slip out of handcuffs.) The ship was but a few miles outbound when he slipped his shackles, forced open the door of his prison and furtively made his way to the upper deck. Hiding himself in an empty compartment he planned his next move. He knew he had to get off the ship for he would be missed shortly and once the ship made open water he would have no chance to swim to land. The question was how to manage that task.

The sea at that point was one of strong tides and cross currents. Still, he reasoned, it would be better to chance freedom while risking death than to stay aboard and go to jail for many years. Whiskey peddlers were harshly dealt with; jail terms up to ten years were common. He knew luck was with him in one important way: the ship was making slow headway through a narrow stretch of water less than a mile from a sizeable island, probably Calvert; and he had customers there who would help him for a promise of a future gift of whiskey.

132

Lucanage made his way to the upper deck then jumped into the cold water. He probably regretted his rash decision the instant he hit the water but survival is a very strong instinct. A good swimmer, he struck out for shore with hard, sweeping strokes.

It was then that he was favored by Lady Luck a second time. The SS *Langley*, a coastal freighter that made regularly scheduled runs from southern B.C. ports to Alaska, was on her northern route. She broke across the horizon a few minutes after Lucanage plunged into the water.

Whether Lucanage would have succeeded in attaining the island became a moot point for he was spotted in the water by a sharp-eyed lookout on the *Langley*'s bridge. The ship was quickly stopped and he was hauled aboard. Taken quickly to the ship's galley he was given warm blankets and a mug of hot soup. Later he was taken to the bridge where the captain asked the usual questions.

What Lucanage told the ship's captain is unknown but he probably told him his fishing boat had sunk. At any rate the captain had no idea his newest passenger was a fugitive so he told him to return to the galley to continue drying his sodden clothes and get some more hot soup.

The next day, May 6, the *Langley* approached the dock at Bella Coola. Lucanage was horrified to see Ogilvie among those on the wharf awaiting the ship's arrival. He quickly went to the outboard side of the ship, waited until the vessel bumped against the pier, then jumped once again into the cold water, swam a few hundred feet then waded ashore. As he pulled himself onto the bank, he could see Ogilvie striding up the gangplank.

Lucanage knew now that his escape would be reported because the captain would certainly inform Ogilvie of the swimmer he had rescued. He could also be certain that Ogilvie would recognize him from the captain's and others' descriptions. He hurried into the town bent only on escape.

What happened next—or even why it happened—is unclear because the fugitive was for all intents and purposes, a free man. He certainly had time to return to the hotel and retrieve the money he had deposited in the safe. From there he could have boarded his boat, still moored in the harbor and sailed to freedom; or, just as easily, he could have headed into the bush and disappeared. Perhaps he dared not risk being seen by the hotel staff. Whatever his reasons, he decided to postpone his escape long enough to go after Ogilvie.

Somehow, undoubtedly by theft, Lucanage acquired a pistol and a knife. He then returned to the dock. The *Langley* was loading cargo so he used the milling dock workers as a cover to slip aboard unseen. Seeing Ogilvie on the ship's bridge talking with the captain he silently made his way to the bridge and peered around the partly open door. He saw the lawman had his back to the door. Lucanage then cocked the pistol, eased open the door and emptied the gun into the policeman's back.

Ogilvie staggered forward but did not fall. Instead he turned and hurled himself against Lucanage. Holding tightly he tried to wrestle the smaller man to the deck but the desperate killer drew his knife and stabbed the police officer several times. Ogilvie slumped to the deck as Lucanage bolted from the ship.

Ogilvie, though mortally wounded, lived long enough to tell who had killed him. The alarm was sounded and within an hour a large group of well-armed townsmen fanned out in several directions to search the woods. They returned hours later to report that not a trace had been found that would point in which direction Antoine Lucanage had fled.

A few days later the government issued a thousand-dollar reward for the assailant, an extremely large amount of money for those days. Suddenly everyone was looking for the fugitive.

Though Lucanage escaped he was forced to remain in hiding, not only because of the large reward ($1000 would support a man for a long time in 1865 when a good wage was about $250) but because the killing of a lawman was considered a most villainous act by the citizenry. With every citizen and not a few bounty hunters watching for him he dare not show his face even to his friends for the reward meant even his gang members, if reports of a gang were true, could never be trusted. Any one of them would have betrayed him for such a reward.

Lucanage dropped from sight completely but rumors of his whereabouts kept cropping up. At one point he was reported as having been seen in California. None of the reports, however, came close to producing the man. Then, late that year, a battered corpse was found floating in the cold water of a northern Vancouver Island inlet. It was easily identified as Lucanage and there was absolutely no doubt he had been murdered. He had been savagely stabbed and clubbed to death.

No one knows for certain how Antoine Lucanage met his grisly demise but the evidence points to a settling of a debt unpaid for that is how such accounts between thieves and outlaws were usually settled in the wild west. Because of the manner in which he had been killed police drew the conclusion, in all likelihood correct, that he had enlisted a couple of his customers to help him escape. He likely promised blankets and whiskey upon his safe return to his island hideout. For one reason or another he didn't produce the payment. Had he forgotten that he was out of alcohol? Had his partners cleaned out his cache of goods? Whatever the reason he could not pay the agreed amount and was savagely killed then dumped into the sea. Obviously his executioners didn't know about the reward for they never claimed it.

Antoine Lucanage was buried in an unmarked grave in an unknown place.

John Ogilvie was buried with full police honors befitting a dedicated lawman.

CHAPTER 13

The Angel of the Goldfields

NELLIE CASHMAN
- ◆ b. Ireland, 1850
- ◆ d. Victoria, B.C., January 4, 1925

Nellie Cashman was one of those rare Old West women who made her mark on history without the stigma of a "Calamity Jane" or the notoriety of a Belle Starr. She made her mark in a manner unusual to the time and places in which she lived. She lived to a good old age and when she did at last shuffle off this mortal coil she left behind many mourners and an array of friends numbering in the hundreds. Among her friends were good people and bad people— and all loved her. She knew such diverse lawmen as Wyatt Earp and Sam Steele of the NWMP plus a large number who stood between the two extremes. Among her acquaintances were the gamblers "Doc" Holliday and Luke Short. "Buckskin Frank" Leslie dined in her Tombstone cafe as did Sheriff John Behan. The good food she served during that town's riotous heyday attracted many customers among whom were Johnny Ringo and "Curly Bill" Brocius, both notorious gunmen. Nellie Cashman knew them all and her name is still enshrined in the history of Arizona.

But it was in British Columbia that she really began her claim to lasting fame and it was there she gained her soubriquet—The Angel of the Goldfields. From there she moved northward to the Yukon and then to Alaska bringing with her the reputation she had earned and expanding on her legend as the years went by.

Nellie was born in Ireland but left to seek a better life when she was sixteen. Following a harrowing sea voyage she arrived in New

York although the date of debarkation is uncertain. She was accompanied by an older sister, Frances, known informally as Fannie. Fannie was probably no older than eighteen. The girls did not stay long in New York for both had decided their futures lay in the developing west.

The two young ladies crossed the continent in the rough conveyances of the era, a long, difficult trip that must have at times filled them with self-doubt as to the wisdom of their venture. However, both girls were determined and Annie may even have enjoyed the hardships. Certainly the trip across the country was nothing to the hardships she was to endure over the next fifty years.

When the pair finally arrived in California, they had been on the road more than six months. The new year was already several weeks old when they stepped off the stage onto the mean streets of San Francisco. (Despite San Francisco's notorious history, the ratio of good women to the bad, dishonest women was four to one. The girls quickly obtained honest employment, settled down, and might have spent the rest of their lives in California had Fannie not fallen in love with a man who remains known only as Mr. Cunningham. He and Fannie were married whereupon she abandoned any thoughts she might have had for further adventure. The marriage appears to have been long and happy. Although little is known of Fannie Cunningham's eventual fate, she did have at least one son who settled in Arizona and whose descendants are still there.

Nellie, with her perky look and fresh complexion commonplace to Irish lasses, was a strikingly pretty teenager. She met any number of eager young men, some well-to-do, most of whom were seeking a wife. She received a number of serious proposals but she politely turned them all aside. Nellie had her own agenda and it did not include early marriage. Having decided to become a wealthy woman in her own right, she had one thing on her mind and that was to amass a fortune. Until she had attained that goal, she had decided not to consider such a thing as marriage. She was still only eighteen. She did, however, remain in San Francisco for four more years living as a boarder with Fannie and her husband.

Her six years in San Francisco were not spectacular for there is no mention of her outside of the city registry that recorded all residents—or as many residents as could be located. Annie reenters western history in 1872, the year she went to Virginia City, Nevada. There in that roaring town she opened a restaurant. It was not a cafe in the strict sense of the word. Basically it was a small, short-order room but her cooking was so good the business flourished with the result the place was always crowded.

By 1874, Virginia City was almost mined out but silver had been discovered in Arizona at a place called Tombstone. Annie packed her equipment and moved to Tombstone where she started another cafe, this one a bigger place able to accommodate many patrons without the overcrowding that had plagued her patience in Nevada.

Nellie did extremely well in Tombstone. Her frugal habits and good business sense allowed her to amass a small fortune, which she salted away with her Nevada profits. She could see, though, that Tombstone would not last forever as a boom town, so before it began to flounder Nellie decided the time had come to move on. She decided to sell the cafe and head north. (The Nellie Cashman Cafe is now one of the many tourist attractions in Tombstone.)

Having heard of the good gold strikes in the Cassiar District of British Columbia, she decided to try her hand at moiling for gold. She sold her cafe for a tidy sum, journeyed to San Francisco then took a ship to Victoria. Most gold seekers went first to Victoria to outfit themselves before ferrying across to the mainland and hence north. Annie decided to follow that route and it was while she was in Victoria that an incident occurred which would change not only her life but her outlook on life.

While in Victoria, Annie came into contact with a group of Catholic nuns who were struggling to establish a hospital as an addition to a school they had founded three years before. The school was proving itself so successful that a great number of its students were of different denominations. Parents, liking the rigid discipline imposed by the nuns, decided it was an ideal place to send their children. The hospital, however, was having a difficult beginning for some reason.

The nuns was working extremely hard to get their latest idea out of the blocks and running. Nellie, who admired initiative and determination, praised her new acquaintances' zeal and dedication. She contributed some of her Tombstone profits toward their goal before leaving for the Cassiar. Her gesture was the start of a lifelong friendship.

Nellie arrived at a mining camp near Dease Lake, took a good long look at the situation and immediately decided she could make a fortune by handling two businesses at the same time. She would accommodate the culinary needs of miners and work a claim simultaneously. She was never one to doubt her abilities but she realized she could not work a restaurant and a mine at the same time. Restaurants take too much of the owner's time.

Shunning the idea of the restaurant Nellie opened a boardinghouse instead. It was quickly filled with miners who appreciated good cooking. Once the house was well established, she hired some dependable help to run the place and departed into the bush, pick, shovel and gold pan in hand. When she returned days later, she had laid several claims.

With her boardinghouse going full tilt and her claims producing reasonable amounts of gold Nellie made a trip to Victoria. She had become alarmed at what she had seen in her travels through the bush. She had observed the unmistakable signs of scurvy among an alarming number of miners. When she returned from Victoria it was with six hired men all hauling and heaving huge wagons filled with vegetables and large hogsheads of lime and lemon juice. What made the 720-mile trek (1120 km) truly amazing is that it had been accomplished in the dead of winter along rugged trails which were barely passable at the best of times. Nellie was glowingly praised by her hired men for working as hard as any them. Her legend began at this point.

Nellie and her crew arrived in the proverbial nick of time, for when the group arrived at Dease Lake seventy-five miners were in varying stages of scurvy with some close to death. All would have perished had not Nellie nursed them back to health. She charged not a single penny for the food she dispensed to those men.

She continued to use some, actually a great deal, of her mining profits to do humanitarian work among the miners. She never took a penny in payment, not even offers of donations would she accept. She dismissed such offers by stating she felt she should repay some of her own good fortune to those who needed some help.

How much of her time was spent nursing sick miners has never been determined but it is known to have been considerable. Miners returning south told of this unusual woman. Soon her efforts in the Cassiar goldfields gained for her a far-reaching fame. As word filtered back to southern newspapers, she became highly prized as a subject for human interest articles.

While few reporters were shy about asking personal questions, she countered their enquiries with demure replies that managed to titillate the readers. Nellie had a sense of humor and knew how to play the press, which she did magnificently. Nonetheless, there was never a doubt that she would not allow the rough-hewn miners to get too close. As she later admitted she had no fear for her virtue because the miners themselves had come to look on her as some sort of special person sent by providence to care for them along the way. In fact, they protected her by keeping a vigilant eye on her.

Nellie became well known throughout B.C. as she worked her way from one goldfield to another, laying claims, panning gold and helping sick miners back to health. In Victoria, where she spent some time each winter, she became a light of society and was much in demand as an honored guest. She kept her contacts with her friends, the nuns, becoming a leading benefactor to their now well-established hospital.

In 1898, now forty-eight, Nellie joined the gold rush to the Klondike where she endured the hardships of the journey through and over the Chilkoot Pass and a dreadful winter at Lake Laberge, the lake made famous by Robert Service and his fictional hero Sam McGee.

Arriving by raft at Dawson City Nellie opened a cafe, a hotel and a grocery store. She set up a reading room in the hotel where lonely men could read and write letters home. She also laid a claim that ultimately netted her a princely $100,000 profit (at least one million dollars by today's standards). She also held several small claims that showed healthy profits. Nellie was in Dawson City when Inspector Sam Steele of the NWMP faced down Soapy Smith, the notorious scam artist and gunfighter and sent him, thoroughly chastened, skulking back to Alaska and his final, fatal gunfight. Smith was shot to death by Frank Reid in a gunfight in Skagway in June, 1898. He was thirty-eight.

Nellie Cashman eventually made her home permanently in the north. From Dawson City she went to Fairbanks then to the inland community of Koyukuk, only 500 miles from the Arctic Circle becoming in the process the first white woman to venture so far north.

Nellie became the owner/operator of no fewer than eleven profitable mines. She always considered the Dawson claim her flagship, probably because it was the most profitable. She traveled between her mines by dog team, canoe, barge and raft. During those travels she spent much time and no small part of her now-vast fortune bringing medicine and nursing skills to sick miners. At age seventy-two she pushed a team of huskies on a grueling 720-mile (1120 km) run across Alaska on a mission of mercy.

However, the years of toil had taken a toll. In 1923, the year after her great dogsled trek across Alaska, she went into a hospital at Fairbanks suffering from pneumonia. Upon her release she realized the cold northern winters were becoming too much for her. Her doctor advised her to go south for the healing warmth of the sun. She made plans to go to Arizona for the remainder of the winter and perhaps arrange to go there each winter thereafter. Her nephew, Fannie's son, lived in Bisbee and he convinced her she would fare better there during winter than in Alaska.

Nellie took shipboard passage to Victoria but that was as far as she got. While at sea, she suffered a relapse of pneumonia. When the ship docked at Victoria she was taken ashore for hospitalization in St. Joseph's Hospital, the very one she had been so instrumental in founding. The nurses there did their best to affect a cure but Nellie Cashman had grown too weak to respond to treatment. For days she drifted in and out of consciousness.

During lucid moments she told several of the nurses that she was very tired and thought it about time to depart this world because she wanted to "...get together up there with all the fellows I used to know." She would then nod her head skywards before continuing. "We'll do some minin' sure enough and spin some yarns about the good days and maybe even a few about them that was not so good."

On January 4, 1925, Nellie Cashman, the perky Irish lass, frontier woman extraordinary, gold miner and angel of the gold fields, died while in a peaceful sleep. Her friends, and there were many, attended her funeral. She is buried in the Ross Bay Cemetery in Victoria. She rests among the nuns she helped in their efforts to build the hospital that was in operation until a few years ago. Her grave is on the route of the organized tours for which the cemetery is famed.

CHAPTER 14

Sudden Death—
Vigilante Style

CHARLES "ONE EAR" BROWN
* b. Unknown
* d. Washington Territory, April, 1867

Where Charlie Brown, if that was indeed his real name, came from is not known for certain. He is believed by some to have been an American badman and by others to have had his origins in eastern Canada. He may well have been a home-grown B.C. product. No one can say for certain. There have been, after all, many people named Charles Brown but very few of the lowlife type that describes our Charlie Brown. This particular Brown was bad through and through, had absolutely no redeeming qualities, was totally lacking in principles and decency and can be held largely responsible for the decimation of the Songhee Indian band of southern Vancouver Island.

Our Charlie Brown entered western history without fanfare on the day in 1859 when he arrived in Victoria, B.C. He left it violently the morning four vigilantes gunned him down on a lonely section of the old Walla Walla Trail about twenty-seven miles north of Bonner's Ferry, Washington Territory. (This area is now Idaho.) In the eight years between those two eventful days in his life he made a living selling illegal alcohol to the Songhee Indians, spent months in the Victoria jail, escaped to the New Westminster area, stole horses, spent more time in jail, staged a few minor holdups of small trading posts, disappeared for some time then, in his final crime spree, stole a horse and murdered a police officer.

Brown had been in Victoria only a few weeks when he first

came to the notice of the police. That was the day he was arrested for alcohol peddling, a business rampant in Victoria in 1859. It cost very little to buy pure grain alcohol, which was available in five gallon cans from local drug stores. Any number of cans would be sold to any white man for about twenty cents a gallon. These unconscionable men then mixed the spirit with water to increase the volume. Because the water diminished the alcohol's ability to blaze into flame, something had to be added to make the alcohol burn. In order to ensure a good blaze the peddlers added a liberal dose of Camphene, a volatile oil made from turpentine. That restored the alcohol's ability to flame readily. Some peddlers added a touch too much whereupon when being tested for burning power, the Camphene would explode. On those occasions the "burning power" of the mixture was sufficient to set fire to nearby buildings. Several peddlers were badly burned in these explosions from time to time.

As mentioned in previous chapters, the peddlers would also add red dye to give the alcohol the same tint as that of legitimately distilled rye whiskey. In order to give the brew a ryelike "bite" Jamaican ginger was added. Thus doctored, a gallon of straight alcohol could be diluted to three gallons and the kick remained potent. The Indians, already ravaged by the white mens' small pox, measles and assorted diseases against which they had no immunity, were further poisoned by this evil potion inflicted upon them by men such as Charlie Brown. The Songhee band, once the dominant group in the area, was almost wiped out by the whiskey traders. Charlie "One Ear" Brown can be held personally responsible for much of that devastation.

So great was the demand for the blighted brew an Indian would pay exorbitant amounts in cash, furs and other valuable items. But the real cost was the eradication the illegal substance was exacting against them. Alcohol was a forbidden substance for Natives and selling it to them was considered a very serious offense. Despite harsh penalties, there flourished a brisk trade in the nefarious business.

Charlie Brown, a man bereft of ethics and morals, immediately saw what profits could be had. He bought several cans of alcohol and began hustling along the waterfront. His business flourished and he sold more and more until he had a sizeable amount of money stashed away. On several occasions he was arrested and fined as much as $500. Each time he paid the fines in cash and walked away from the courthouse at Bastion Square to return directly to the waterfront where he continued in his pursuits. He seems to have been undeterred by the hefty fines.

Brown obviously tried the patience of the court once too often for on November 3, 1859, he was not given the option of a fine but was sentenced by a Victoria magistrate to a jail term of hard labor. He had grown so bold he was caught in plain view of the police selling "whiskey" to an Indian woman directly from a tin right on Yates Street, one of Victoria's main thoroughfares. He spent the next six months breaking large boulders into tiny pieces of gravel thus contributing in a small way to the building of Victoria's downtown streets.

Released in May, 1860, Brown was a free man for less than two weeks before he was again arrested. This charge was for swindling a fur trader. He was quickly sent back to the chain gang for another six months.

Brown, never a model prisoner, could not stay out of trouble in jail so he spent most of the sentence locked in his cell with bread and water his only nourishment. He gained no remission. After serving his full term he was freed in November; but by mid-1861 he was already halfway through yet another term for a similar offense. The last sentence, handed down in December, had been one of twelve months. It was during this 1861 term he gained the nickname that assured him a place in the annals of the Canadian wild west.

Charles B. Wright, a guard, had been told to move Brown from one cell to another. Brown balked and threatened to kill Wright if he entered the cell.

"You come through that door you son-of-a-bitch and I'll kill you," Brown snarled.

Wright, not one to be intimidated by such as Charlie Brown, swung the door open and entered the cell.

"Pick up your gear and come with me," Wright ordered.

"Go to hell," Brown replied, and with escape on his mind, charged the burly jailer, grasped him in a bear hug and attempted to hurl him against the wall.

Wright managed to draw his pistol and got his arm into a position where the muzzle of the gun was jammed alongside Brown's head. Wright ordered Brown to release his grip. Brown, defiantly, squeezed harder. Wright pulled the trigger.

The pistol, a large-caliber revolver, roared amidst a billow of smoke and flame. The slug, driven by forty-four grains of black powder, blasted away Brown's left ear. Flame from the black powder set his hair afire and burned the side of his face and head. In all likelihood it also cauterized the wound. It also settled the issue of whether Brown had any fight left in him.

Wright dragged Brown to his new cell, threw him to the floor, locked the door then went to the office to call a doctor and file a charge of attempting to escape lawful custody. A local doctor was duly summoned and he patched Brown's wounds.

The following morning Brown was brought into court to face two new charges—attempting to escape and assaulting a guard. His bandages, missing ear and singed hair garnered him no sympathy from the judge who promptly awarded him another full year—to begin upon completion of the year he was already serving.

Brown, for all his faults, was not a quitter. Every night, and probably through all his days, he spent his time plotting ways to escape. One night he hit upon a plan he considered fail proof. He would escape by feigning illness. Having nothing left to lose he decided to put the idea into motion the very next day.

Brown dutifully broke rocks all morning while waiting for the noon break. He ate his meager lunch then suddenly stood up, began to sway and complain of a dizziness which was overcoming him. Then he clutched his midsection, groaned and keeled over. When he "came to" a few minutes later, he appeared groggy and complained of a severe aching in his gut. His act was good enough to convince his jailers that he was in great agony. He was quickly transported to the city hospital. He was pleased; so far the plan was working.

Brown stayed in bed biding his time until that night when he slipped away and was gone. Somehow, he made his way over to the mainland, stole a horse near Chilliwack and was promptly caught. The stolen horse earned him a stint in the penitentiary at New Westminster. There he was confined to serve out the remainder of his Victoria sentence as well as a further two years on the latest charge.

Released at the end of his sentence, probably late 1865, he disappeared. He may have gone to the United States, although no records exist indicating he was ever on Washington Territory's wanted lists. No posters describing a one-eared suspect have been found. If he stayed in B.C. he either behaved himself or at least was not caught doing anything, the latter being the most likely.

Brown reenters history in April, 1867, the month he showed up near Colville, in what is now Washington State, at the Kootenay Trading Station, an outpost a few miles south of the border. It was a time when men were traveling freely across the border heading to or returning from the gold strikes in the mountains and the Kootenay Valley north of Cranbrook. Normally no one paid much attention to these pilgrims. Each one looked very much like all the others.

However, a man with only one ear was hard to overlook so Charlie Brown was noticed—and remembered—by several people because of his habit of talking loudly and boastfully of feats he insisted he had accomplished. Also noticed was the arsenal he carried. It ranged from a heavy-bore rifle to a pair of large-caliber pistols to a wide-blade skinning knife. He made a habit of bragging of his marksmanship and his willingness to use his weapons. Such a man was hard to overlook.

Apparently Brown had lost none of his other bad habits either for when he left the trading station he promptly stole two horses from a nearby ranch. The ranch was owned by two brothers, recent immigrants from Holland. (As is often the case in Old West history, one version of Charlie Brown's story says the ranch was owned by a Scotsman. Regardless, the article doesn't dispute that Brown stole the horses.) He was observed as he rode out of the corral but was gone before the brothers could challenge him. Their delay probably saved their lives.

The brothers, either because they were new to the territory and naive or very brave, did not report the theft to the nearest sheriff. Instead, they wasted no time in saddling up and riding after the thief. Following two horses when one is being led is never a difficult chore so they had little trouble following the trail. The track led the pair into Canada. A few miles further north they discovered a camp about four miles from Wild Horse, a small mining camp town not far from Wild Horse Creek. They reigned up, took a look and saw their horses tied to a tree. There was no sign of the thief, but the two felt uneasy and did not approach closer.

Discretion now took over and the two rode into Wild Horse to report the theft and give the location of the thief's camp. They located a young constable, Jack Lawson of the B.C. Police. Lawson was the only lawman in the town that day as he had been left to tend to the detachment's paper work while the two other officers went on patrol. The ranchers told Lawson their story.

Inexperienced, basically a raw recruit, the young constable felt capable enough to accompany the brothers and help them retrieve their horses. The three rode from town but had not gone far when Brown, astride one of the horses and leading the other, rounded a bend in the trail. Lawson called on him to stop. Brown, with no escape route handy, did as requested.

Lawson then questioned Brown about the horses but while so doing noticed Brown's hand inching toward a holster on his gunbelt. The officer drew his pistol and ordered Brown to stretch his arms high above his head and dismount—slowly. Brown complied. Lawson informed Brown that he was under arrest. The young lawman called to his companions that one should dismount and cover Brown with a rifle while he handcuffed his prisoner. It was at that point that Lawson's inexperience betrayed him. He carelessly took his eyes off his prisoner when he addressed the brothers. In that singular moment Brown's right hand flashed downward. In a split second he had drawn his pistol and fired. One shot rang out. Lawson, shot squarely in the head just back of the left ear, slid backwards and sideways from his saddle—dead before he hit the ground.

The two witnesses to the event, thoroughly frightened, spurred their horses and raced at top speed back to Wild Horse. Brown calmly took the constable's pistol, remounted and resumed his journey south.

While Brown cantered toward the border, the brothers reached Wild Horse. There they told their story to a group of miners, gave a good description of the shooter, the horses and the direction in which the killer had fled.

Two miners were sent to find the patrolling constables while arrangements were made to form a posse. No one paid any attention to four men who had stood at the edge of the crowd listening intently to the excited brothers' tale. Neither did anyone notice when they left the group.

The four went directly to the livery stable, hurriedly saddled their horses, checked the shotguns in their saddle sheaths and buckled on their gun belts. They rode quietly out of town along the trail leading to the border.

The four riders knew Brown had a good three-hour lead on them but they quickly discovered that the man with one ear was not making very good time and he was close at hand. They had come across an Indian trapper leading two horses matching the description of those stolen. The Indian told them he took the horses in hand when a man with one ear abandoned them near the bank of the St. Mary River. The trapper said the man had transferred all his gear from the horses to a raft he had found. He had then attempted to cross the river on the raft but had not gone far before the raft upset in the rapids. The man and all his supplies had been dumped into the swirling waters. The one-eared man managed to swim to the opposite shore, the trapper told them, and after a short rest proceeded on foot toward a mining camp. The trapper said the camp was that of a placer miner named Joe Davis. The trapper was advised to take the horses directly to the police at Wild Horse as they were stolen animals.

The four obviously knew the terrain for they rode some distance downstream to a point where the river could be crossed safely. Urging their mounts across the cold, swift-flowing river, they back-trailed the short distance to Joe Davis' camp.

When the four riders approached the camp Davis met them. They told him they were trailing a man with one ear. Davis was all cooperation. He replied that a short while earlier he had given a one-eared man a small amount of food. He had also asked for ammunition for his weapons but Davis had no shells in the required caliber. The man then departed on the trail leading south.

The next stop was at a Chinese miner's cabin where the men were told their quarry had asked for ammunition. The Chinese man had none to give so Brown moved on. A few miles further the riders came upon a very small settlement. There it was revealed that a one-eared man had stopped at the forge of the village blacksmith. He asked for rifle and pistol ammunition but the smithy had told him he had none to give. The man, obviously thinking the smithy was lying, had become belligerent. He bragged that he had just killed a lawman and had no qualms about shooting the smithy if he discovered shells in the shack. The smithy said the fellow had then looked around but found none and had departed. The smithy told the men their quarry had departed about two hours before.

The time lapses were growing decidedly shorter so the trackers knew Brown was still afoot. They also felt certain he would not stay on the trail if he heard the sound of approaching horses but would seek refuge several yards into the woods. They knew they were likely to ride past him and thus miss him. This would not be a bad idea as then the fugitive would be behind them. Let him come to us, they decided.

They concluded they could safely push their mounts a little

harder, proceed to Bonner's Ferry and there they could spend the night without fear of Brown's gaining in distance. The four rode directly to Bonner's Ferry, settled their mustangs in a livery stable then enjoyed a good supper at a cafe. They then returned to the stable where they spent the night. It was common practice in the days of the old west for a traveler to spend the night with his horse. For an extra charge of ten to twenty-five cents it was cheaper than a hotel ($1) and the horse could be watched. The only rule was a promise not to smoke within the confines of the barn.

The following morning, before the sun was up, they saddled their horses and, feeling certain that they were indeed ahead of the fugitive, headed on a backtrack toward the border.

Spotting an Indian walking toward Bonner's Ferry they hailed him and asked the usual questions. The Indian replied that the previous evening he had been accosted by a white man with one ear. The man had asked for food and ammunition but he had nothing to give and had moved on. The one-eared man, however, had remained behind. The Indian felt he was intending to make camp for the night. He also affirmed that the man they sought was heavily armed.

The four were elated. They now knew they had their quarry where they wanted him. They dismounted and led their horses well off the trail where they tethered them. One of the quartet stayed with the horses while the others returned to the trail. Walking quietly north a few hundred feet, they stationed themselves just off the trail under cover of an aspen grove. There they awaited their man.

Charlie "One Ear" Brown had experienced a very difficult journey. He had lost all his supplies when the raft capsized in the rapids. Though he had managed to save his rifle and pistols, including the one he had taken from the dead lawman, his spare ammunition had gone to the bottom. The remaining ammunition had gotten so wet it was useless. Without the means with which to shoot a small animal for food he had no way of obtaining meat. The time of year was such that ripe, edible berries were not yet available. The April nights were cold and the possibility of encountering a hungry bear was always worrisome, especially so to a man with no shells in his gun. Charlie Brown, cold, hungry and dog tired pulled his tattered clothing as high around his neck as he could and tried to get some badly needed sleep.

The following morning Brown struggled to his feet. He lurched out of the brush onto the trail. He had not slept. The night had been too cold for sleep. His feet were sore from walking, something he did not do often. He knew he was safe, though, and he was thankful for that. He had killed the lawman in Canada and now that he was south of the border he was well out of the reach of Canadian authorities. He pushed himself forward. As soon as he could find a homestead he could steal a horse and some food. Perhaps he could hold up some remote way-station and get some cash. Then he would head for Montana. A man could easily get lost in that rambling territory.

While Charlie Brown was stumbling along the trail forming his plans for his immediate future, the vigilantes were sitting quietly in their thicket. They did not speak or make any sound. All eyes were kept on the trail. They had a view of several hundred feet. No one could approach from the north without being seen moments before they drew near. They did not have long to wait.

The sun was not very high in the morning sky when they saw the one-eared man furtively approaching, tracking carefully along the far edge of the trail. Every so often he stopped to look northward as if half expecting to see trackers approaching from the rear. He may have felt safe but he was not intending to walk on the wrong side of caution. Brown, his mind on whatever might be coming from the north, walked right into the well-laid trap.

The vigilantes saw immediately that their quarry was armed. They noted the rifle, the pistols at his belt and the skinning knife in his left hand. They allowed Charlie Brown to come into range then, stepping out from their place of concealment, blasted him with all the power of three double-barreled shotguns. The blasts hit him full frontal. The shot ripped into his innards, tore away his face and nearly severed one arm from the shoulder. Brown reeled backwards as if punched by a gigantic battering ram. He was dead before he hit the ground.

The vigilantes, who had been the man's trackers, his jury, his judge and finally his executioners then became his undertakers. They dug a shallow grave just off the trail, marked its location carefully so it could be found by anyone looking specifically for it then they buried Charlie "One Ear" Brown. Perhaps one read a short prayer. Perhaps not. Retrieving their horses they rode north to Wild Horse returning no less quietly than they had departed.

Some days later an anonymous letter addressed to the editor was delivered to *The British Columbian*, the New Westminster newspaper. The letter detailed how Brown had met his death. It outlined directions for locating the grave should anyone want to claim the body. No one ever came forward. The newspaper published the letter and wrote a side article on Charlie Brown for he was well known to the law in the New Westminster area. The letter was turned over to the B.C. authorities.

Canadian authorities were not at all interested in the remains of Charlie Brown. The official reason was that the killing had been carried out in American territory. Therefore, it was an American matter for the law of Washington Territory to deal with. Not so, replied the Americans. They were not in the least interested because they considered Brown to be Canadian. Therefore, he was not entitled to be reburied at the expense of American taxpayers.

The citizens of Wild Horse had no interest in his remains as he was not of their society. They were happy to be rid of another outlaw. The B.C. Police, following a routine investigation, announced no further inquiry could be made because there were no witnesses to the killing and no one could, or would, divulge the identities of the vigilantes. However, the B.C. Police did agree the case should remain open as unsolved. Presumably it still is on the books. Presumably, also, in his shallow grave Charlie "One Ear" Brown remains to this day in quiet repose under a canopy of shading alders within a few feet of a long forgotten trail. Ironically, because the vigilantes shot Brown in Idaho, it did not spoil B.C.'s reputation as never having a vigilante-style execution.

CHAPTER 15

The Shootout at Fortier's Café

◆ Fisherville, B.C. (August 9, 1864)

Fisherville was a town built in a hurry. It sprang up almost overnight along the banks of Wild Horse Creek, one of hundreds of narrow rivulets that flow quietly along ages-old courses from various headwaters in the Rockies. Fisherville was located 300 miles (480 km) east of Vancouver in terrain that can be described only as rough. In 1864 it took twenty days on horseback to cover the distance now achieved by car in less than twelve hours. Fisherville no longer exists but Wild Horse Creek still runs its same path and can be located near a reconstructed ghost town known as Fort Steele, a tourist attraction on Highway 93 between Wasa and Cranbrook.

When gold was discovered in Wild Horse Creek in late 1863 word spread quickly. Within weeks the area was dotted with tents, crude shacks and roughly constructed lean-tos which housed between 5,000 and 6,000 gold-fevered men. By early 1864 the area was a madhouse—and the gold was indeed plentiful. Some miners left after only a couple of months with $40,000 or more in dust and nuggets—a huge fortune in those days.

The shanty town, which for no discernable reason was called Fisherville, was quickly built. By 1864 it had grown from the scattered tents of 1863 to fifty wooden cabins, several large wooden buildings and a great number of so-called "dance halls" that were really saloons where women danced a one-minute whirl-around with the miners for a small fee (usually ten cents) then did their best to convince them to spend larger amounts on drinks. The girls received a generous commission on the liquor they sold.

The brothels were open at all hours as "soiled doves" plied their trade and the gambling tents also operated around the clock. As many saloons as the town could support plus a full-fledged brewery kept everyone well supplied with liquid refreshment. The town had a permanent residency list of about 2,000 men and several dozen women. They owned the saloons, cafes and other businesses that catered to the miners. These men and women dedicated themselves to separating the miners from their gold by any means, legal and otherwise.

The Wild Horse Creek gold rush lasted about three years before dwindling quickly. A few stalwarts remained but after a few more years the last of the miners departed.

However, during its heyday Fisherville was every bit as wide open a town as the roughest mining town anywhere lacking only the murders and stagecoach robberies that made such places as Bear River, Wyoming, or Tombstone, Arizona, so notable. Fisherville achieved two claims to fame. The one was that it was taken completely apart board by board and nail by nail in 1865 when a huge lode of gold ore was discovered directly under its main street. Its second claim to notoriety was the 1864 gun fight on the main street that made the gunfight at Tombstone's OK Corral appear tame.

The gunfight, like that of Tombstone, had its roots in differences of opinion. Whereas Tombstone's differences were that one faction (headed by the Earp brothers) wanted to be the law and their opponents (the Clanton gang) preferred there be no law at all, the Fisherville factions both wanted to represent the town's law. For months the argument raged back and forth and, like Tombstone, it was mostly harsh talk and little serious trouble. The factions sparred back and forth neither wanting to give an inch. That both ended with a gunfight is interesting but coincidental.

The problem with the matter of law and order in Fisherville was simply that the area had no authorized lawmen. The B.C. authorities had been unable to establish a permanent judiciary owing to a lack of judges to hear court cases and constables to keep the peace. Judges were scarce because no successful lawyer wanted to accept such an appointment and trade a practice in a civilized town for the hard trail of a circuit rider. Police officers were equally hard to recruit because the pittance they were paid had no appeal when a few lucky months in the goldfields could make a man a millionaire. Thirty dollars a month and a chance to get shot in the back didn't quite cut it.

What law there was, therefore, would have to be of the home-made variety so the authorities let it be known that vigilance committees would be tolerated so long as no one was hanged. Anything of a serious nature was to be referred to the nearest B.C. Police commander. For Fisherville that meant Nelson, a large town more than 120 miles distant. It took a man on horseback a week to ten days of slogging rough trails and crossing rivers to get there.

In any event the vested authority to keep order was duly assigned to a vigilante group under the leadership of one Robert Dore. Little is known of this individual except that he had aspirations of being named either sheriff or magistrate for the Kootenay District. His group did a commendable job and had success in policing the town.

Dore, however, was an egomaniac. Insisting upon complete control, he interfered with subcommittees and overrode the decisions of "the court." Eventually his vigilance committee split into two factions, one a group of Americans under the leadership of a trio named William "Yeast Powder Bill" Denniston (a.k.a. Bill Burmiester), Robert "Overland Bob" Evans and Neil Dougherty who had no nickname. The opposing faction, mostly Canadians and British, was a decided minority lead by a hot-tempered, vocal Irishman named Thomas "Tom" Walker. His lieutenants were William "Dancing Bill" Latham, John "Black Jack" Smyth and "Paddy" Skie.

The factions could not agree on the way to run the town and tempers were continuously on edge. Where Robert Dore fit into all this no one ever knew, but it is suspected he stood by egging the two factions on from the sidelines. No doubt he hoped to reclaim the pieces after the dust had settled.

The two groups eventually agreed to meet to talk things over in the street outside of Fortier's Cafe during the afternoon of August 9, a particularly hot day. Most of the men were armed with pistols but others held clubs. The two groups faced each other in two rows about thirty feet apart. Walker and Denniston met at a point midway between the two groups. Walker had a .45-caliber pistol at his belt while Yeast Powder Bill wore his customary two guns.

The talk started peacefully enough but within a few minutes the two began shouting. Tom Walker, his temper boiling over, pulled his revolver from its holster, leveled it at Yeast Powder Bill and squeezed the trigger.

The range was point blank when the heavy pistol roared but, unfortunately for Walker, his hand was unsteady. The .45 slug missed Bill's expansive chest but ripped away the thumb from his right hand. Walker tried to fire a second shot but his gun jammed. Yeast Powder Bill, howling in shock and pain, drew the pistol from his left holster and shot Walker through the heart. Walker died where he stood. It was his great bad luck that Bill was ambidextrous.

When Walker's gun fired, Overland Bob Evans commenced shooting. This brought immediate return fire from Walker's friends. Within seconds the shooting had become general and Evans lay prone in the dust with at least two bullets in his body. Although Evans was down his companions, thinking him dead, continued shooting.

Tom Walker was dead, there was no doubt of that, and his friends, intent on avenging him, kept up a steady barrage of fire into the ranks of the Americans. For several minutes the scene was one of sheer chaos. The men who were armed with clubs closed and began to beat on each other. When the shooting finally stopped the air hung heavy with the acrid smell of gun smoke. Both sides retreated to count their casualties.

Walker, it turned out, was the only one confirmed dead. Denniston had a thumbless, severely wounded hand. It was bandaged and he lurched away to a nearby saloon for a solid shot of painkiller. Bob Evans was so badly shot up he was considered as good as dead. He was carried to his tent, placed on his bedroll and left to die. Surprisingly he survived, but three months passed before he regained his feet. Paddy Skie, of the Walker faction, had taken a bullet in the head. He also was carried to his tent, placed on his cot and left to die. A few friends stayed to tend to him during his last minutes but when he did not pass on they departed. He could, they figured, die on his own when the time came.

But Paddy Skie did not die although he lay in a coma for more than four months. One morning he suddenly opened his eyes, rose unsteadily from his bed, tottered on wobbly legs out of the tent to a small group of men standing nearby and enquired as to what in hell had happened. They told him. One led him back to his tent while another hurried to Fortier's café to fetch him a cup of hot soup. A few days later, seemingly fully recovered, he returned to his claim, hit a small but rich lode and lived a number of years more without further complications.

Among the wounded, a man identified only as Kelly, was discovered bleeding in the dusty road with a knife protruding from his back. He, too, recovered after some weeks on his cot.

Once the gun smoke had dispersed and the casualties counted the survivors from both sides, shaken and appalled at what had transpired, assembled in peace to determine what to do. They never got the chance because the neutral miners had quickly formed a committee to handle the problem. This new committee decided to first send a couple of riders to Nelson to report the incident to the B.C. Police commander. They then assembled a court to decide on a day to try Yeast Powder Bill and Overland Bob Evans for murdering Walker.

There was no discussion on that decision as it was in keeping with the custom of the day. Following any gunfight the survivor was always tried or at least held pending a coroner's inquest. He was also usually acquitted on grounds of self defense. All he had to do was tell the court of enquiry that his opponent had been the first to reach for a gun. The opponent of course could not dispute the claim so the jury had no other evidence to go on.

The committee appointed A. J. Gregory as judge, named a lawyer to defend Denniston and Evans and set a court date. Then the committee named John McClellan to act as sheriff giving him authority to maintain order with as many deputies as he cared to appoint. Then they sat back to await developments.

McClellan immediately arrested Yeast Powder Bob and lodged him in a makeshift jail. Evans obviously wasn't going anywhere so he was left in his bed.

Several days later the riders who had alerted the authorities at Nelson returned. They told the vigilantes that they must do nothing further until the police arrived. This was met with agreement. However, the committee decided to proceed with the trial on the day they had already set.

On the day before the trial was to commence Commissioner John Carmichael Haynes and Constable William Young rode into town. Young, sitting astride his horse with a rifle lying loosely across the saddle's pommel, informed the assembled miners that he would represent the law from that point onward. While Young was informing the group of his duties, Judge Haynes dismissed the "judge" and the "lawyers." The following morning Haynes assembled a jury of twelve men chosen at random and held an inquest.

The jury, upon hearing the evidence and the testimony from witnesses, agreed that Walker had fired the first shot. Denniston was released and Evans, still on his cot, was informed that no charges would be laid against him.

While the inquest was being held, Young busied himself posting notices informing one and all that in future guns and other weapons were not to be brought into town—and he assured all and sundry that the ordinance would be upheld. Young, a small man who wore a sort of old army uniform complete with "pillbox" hat, was not the flamboyant lawman of the type American cattle towns attracted, but no one had any doubts about his ability to back up his edicts. The pistol at his belt was of a large caliber and he carried his rifle in such a way that there could be no doubts that this man knew how to use it. No one was of a mind to find out if he was or was not a good pistol shot.

Within a week Fisherville became a quiet, well-ordered town. No one except Young carried a gun inside the town limits. The saloons, dance halls, dancing girls, soiled doves and gambling tents all remained as active as ever, but there was never another shooting or act of serious violence within the town's boundaries. There would, however, be another shooting in the area the following year when Constable Jack Lawson was killed by Charlie "One Ear" Brown. That story is told in its own chapter.

CHAPTER 16

The Man Who Started the Gold Rush

JAMES MASON "Skookum Jim"
- b. Yukon Territory, circa 1860
- d. Yukon, 1916

> In the lands of the Tlingit nation
> Up north in the land of the free,
> Skookum's a word that in English means big,
> Just as big as big can be.
>
> "Skookum" fit Jim Mason right to a "T"
> Cause Jim was as big as a Sitka Pine tree,
> And so was his spirit and also his heart,
> Jim Mason was as big as a man could be.
>
> One day Jim was walking along Rabbit Creek
> Making his way through the mist,
> When a glint in the water caught his eye
> And he saw a gold nugget as big as his fist.
>
> So he staked out a claim on old Rabbit Creek
> And ended up with the gold.
> Then he shared his fortune with everyone else.
> At least that's what we have been told.
>
> Now Jim was big not only in size
> But also in spirit and nerve.
> Men started calling him "Skookum Jim"
> 'Twas a name that he richly deserved.
>
> — from "The Ballad of Skookum Jim," *Anon.*

In the Tlingit language "skookum" means strong. But it is one of those Indian words that hold much more meaning than a solitary definition. It also means overwhelming, of good spirit, of generous personality and a wish to help others. Jim Mason fit the description extremely well. From boyhood, even before he gained his soubriquet, he had spent nearly all his time in the woods, trapping for the most part. His life in the woods gave him physique and hard-toned muscles, but it was his generosity toward others and his willingness to extend a helping hand that led to his being called Skookum Jim. He was tough, durable and seemingly tireless. He possessed a capacity for moving through dense bush deemed impassable by lesser men. He was able to paddle his canoe upriver against currents so strong that few could keep up with him. If his companions fell behind he either waited for them or returned to extend assistance. Those who flagged completely he carried out to safety.

Before he was twenty years of age, his reputation had so grown that the name Skookum Jim had became famous throughout the Yukon. As the years passed he became known further afield. He proved to be a dependable and loyal friend. He never had to worry about getting a partner for his ventures. Indeed, it was he who was sought out.

For many years, with two steady partners, he had prospected along a narrow stream known as Rabbit Creek. In 1896 he was walking along the creek's bank when he discovered a large gold nugget. Further inspection of the stream revealed gold in amounts he had never seen before. He hurried to the nearest assayer's office and registered a series of claims in the names of himself and his two partners, claims that ultimately made the trio wealthy. Jim became not only wealthy but famous as the man who started the Klondike gold rush.

He and his partners managed to keep their secret just long enough to stake a number of claims along Rabbit Creek. In 1897 the secret was out—the result was the gold rush.

His discovery also resulted in a change of name for the hitherto obscure creek, although he had nothing to do with that. In fact he was upset by the change. He could not understand why anyone would want to deprive rabbits of the honor of having a creek named after them. Nonetheless, from that year forward the creek would become famed in poetry, song and novels as Bonanza Creek. Jack London and Jack O'Brien, both writers of Yukon novels, set many of their novels along Bonanza Creek. During the 1920s, Hollywood made adventure movies with Bonanza Creek as the setting. Skookum Jim was never to see a movie and one wonders how he would have reacted had he done so. Certainly he would have scoffed at the inaccuracy of such films. While Bonanza Creek became identified with the Yukon in general and the Klondike in particular, neither Hollywood nor the novelists thought to give any credit to the man whose sharp eyes had made it all possible.

By 1898 the area had seen an influx of gold seekers who eventually numbered more than 18,000 plus many hundreds more who followed the seekers to set up saloons, card rooms and other places of entertainment. Fortunately for all concerned, the Canadian government had no intentions of allowing the Klondike to follow the example that had been part and parcel of mining towns south of the border. Determined that the Yukon would not endure the same lawlessness that had bedeviled Montana, Nevada and Arizona, Ottawa ensured a troop of Mounties (under the leadership of the redoubtable Sam Steele) was among the first to arrive. Thus law and order were guaranteed even before the main influx began. Among the newcomers turned away by the Mounties were outlaws such as "Soapy" Smith of Colorado infamy. Skookum Jim never met Smith (Sam Steele personally put the run on the scam artist extraordinaire even before he could clear the checkpoint). The newcomers also included exceptionally good people such as Nellie Cashman, often called the Angel of the Gold Fields. Skookum Jim certainly knew Miss Cashman.

Skookum Jim watched the invasion of his beloved forests and streams with mixed feelings. In many ways he welcomed any influx of money that might help the Tlingit people but in other ways he saw the damage the Yukon area was suffering.

Skookum Jim, as did his partners, became very wealthy but he never forgot his friends be they in the white community or in the Tlingit nation of which he was a very proud member.

Gold gave him wealth but he never exploited it because he never had a great deal of use for it. His first love was trapping. He often said his happiest years were those prior to his discovery of the nugget; and after a couple of years of gold mining, Skookum Jim returned to the life of a trapper. By 1900, when the rush was for all intents and purposes over, he left his mines with his partners and took up full-time trapping.

During the summer months, when trapping was slow, he hired out as a guide for those who wished reliable assistance along the Yukon rivers. He guided surveyors, officials who were required to deal with chiefs of remote Indian villages, worked closely with the NWMP, helped in the trailing of fugitives and became teacher to young Tlingit men who wished to follow in his footsteps.

While Skookum Jim Mason never let his wealth deter him from the work he loved, he allotted much of his time to community life. He worked to better the community until he died, at home in bed, at age fifty-six.

Skookum Jim was one of the proudest Natives who ever lived. Despite the sometimes not so gentle cajoling of missionaries who knew his influence over his people, he refused to completely forsake his belief in the Great Spirit of the Tlingit tenet. He was always quick to give credit to the Frog Spirit whom he said guided him to the spot where he found the nugget that sparked the Klondike rush. He was not even looking for gold the day he found it. He was merely trekking down the trail to meet his sister and brother-in-law when the glint of yellow caught his eye.

When Skookum Jim Mason died, his wishes decreed certain things to be done with the fortune he left. Much of it he left to the Tlingit people to be made available in various ways. His wishes were carried out for the most part although, as is always the case with wills, a certain amount of bickering took its toll. A particularly notable insignia of his legacy is The Skookum Jim Friendship Center, a community center that promotes friendly relations between Native and non-Natives, located in the Yukon city of Whitehorse.

CHAPTER 17

A Most Surprising Verdict

STAR CHILD
- ✦ b. Northwest Territories, circa 1861
- ✦ d. unknown

The Blackfoot nation consisted of three major components: the Siksika, Bloods and Peigans; and two lesser components: Sarsi (or Sarcee) and Atsina (or Gros Ventres). Their language group was Assiniboine. There was no political connection among the various groups but they stayed united through hatred of common enemies.

A famous member of the Blood segment of the Blackfoot nation was Star Child. He was born in the foothills of what is now Alberta. Star Child was perhaps two when the last of the buffalo herds made their final appearance, not yet eight when the whiskey runners arrived with the firewater that would begin the destruction of his people and only thirteen when the arrival of the NWMP marked the beginning of an influx of white farmers and home-steaders onto the prairies. Because his world changed so rapidly, Star Child never learned the art of war, never rode out to hunt the buffalo and did not learn the great traditions of his people. He led an uneventful life until one day in 1879 when, on impulse, he stole a farmer's horse.

Star Child was not a horse thief either by occupation or, at least up to then, inclination. His inexperience betrayed him when he took the animal so brazenly that he was spotted in the act. He was tracked quickly. The horse was recovered and Star Child was arrested and lodged in the jail at Fort MacLeod.

Jail did not suit Star Child at all. The cell was small—too small for an eighteen year old used to the open plains. Not far from his thoughts was the certain knowledge that he faced at least three years of hard labor in the white man's jail. Shoveling out horse stables and breaking large rocks into little ones did not appeal to him. He watched for an opportunity to escape; one afternoon when the guard was distracted, he immediately walked out of the jail and disappeared into the bush. Given the temper of the times, he can hardly be blamed for running; Indians had been shot for lesser crimes than horse theft. He, of course, was well aware of this, but whatever he may have thought of the white man's justice in 1879 he was not prepared for how it would apply to him two years later.

If he lacked talent in stealing horses, Star Child was more than capable of living in the woods. He knew how to hide and for weeks he eluded capture always keeping several steps ahead of the law without ever venturing far afield. He was aided and abetted by friends and relatives all of whom met any questions presented by posse members or investigating police officers with stony silence or an impassive "Don'no" when asked about the young brave.

This wall of silence did not mean the Indians had any great affection for the runaway, it was simply that Natives chose not to go against one of their own people. In all the annals of the west there are very few cases of an Indian being turned in by other Indians, even by those of other tribes. In order to merit betrayal an Indian fugitive had to be thoroughly disliked or without respect within his own tribe. Star Child had not reached that situation.

To the police it appeared that Star Child had never existed, had absolutely no relatives or friends who had ever heard of him or had vanished into thin air. The hunt went on for weeks but slowly decreased until finally only wanted posters pasted to walls on buildings in villages and towns showed him to be a wanted man. That he was not considered dangerous or of significant importance is evidenced by the lack of an offer of even a small reward.

Then, in November, 1879, Constable Marmaduke Graburn of the NWMP came across the elusive one's campsite. Star Child was obviously intending to venture out on a hunting foray for he had already mounted his horse, the same one he had stolen a few weeks before—he had defiantly returned to the scene of his original crime and stole the animal a second time. Constable Graburn certainly didn't consider the young man dangerous because he neither removed his rifle from the saddle scabbard nor did he undo the flap on his pistol holster. He merely rode toward the fugitive intending to place him under arrest. That was a fatal mistake.

Star Child sat in silence astride his horse watching as the constable approached. Whether the Mountie actually called to him or not is unknown. What is known is when Graburn came to within fifty feet of the motionless Indian he suddenly found himself facing the muzzle of a rifle. It was too late for any kind of evasive action. The weapon barked once and Graburn slipped from his saddle a bullet in his chest. As the constable lay dying, Star Child calmly turned his horse away, kicked the animal in the ribs and cantered away to the south. He knew what he had done, what the consequences would be and that he would be safe in Montana.

The body of Constable Graburn was found the next day. Although there were no witnesses, the police had no doubts about the identity of the shooter. Star Child had left enough evidence to indicate he had been at the site. The horse he had stolen had metal shoes of a unique design. Some items known to belong to Star Child had been left at the campsite.

A small posse was formed, but after two days the tracking had become difficult. Nonetheless, sufficient tracks were spotted to indicate clearly that the fugitive had ridden south then crossed over into Montana. There was no point in continuing the chase. All that could be done was wait. Sooner or later Star Child would grow lonesome for the foothills and return. The NWMP had learned much about Indians in their six years of patrolling the prairies. An Indian, they had learned, held great fondness for the place of his or her birth. The land pulled on them like a magnet. Star Child, they knew, would not stay in Montana.

The search for the young brave (he was not yet twenty) was placed on hold while the police turned their attentions to other pressing problems. A rumor was quietly started to the effect that no one was looking for him. It was allowed to make its way into the reservations and, as rumors are prone to do, it spread.

A year later, believing himself safe, Star Child returned quietly to Alberta. He may have heard the rumor or perhaps he had merely grown homesick. Whatever his reason, he made his way back into more familiar hills. He was, he felt, among friends again.

In fact, Star Child did not have quite as many friends as he may have thought. His killing of Grabeck, who had been liked by the Indians, had not gone down well at all with the Bloods. Stealing a horse was one thing but murder was a different matter. Within a few days the police began receiving information that Star Child had come home. Four police officers, acting on those tips, rode out of Fort MacLeod one morning with one purpose in mind—they were to find Star Child's trail. By a stroke of luck he was still riding the stolen horse. Following the unusual hoof marks the four quickly tracked him to a camp not far from Fort MacLeod. With four rifles facing him, Star Child meekly surrendered.

Star Child was duly charged with murdering a police officer and in October, 1881, the trial commenced in Fort MacLeod. Under the normal circumstances prevalent in the west of those days the average trial lasted one day. Star Child's trial followed that schedule almost to the minute. Both sides presented their cases. The judge instructed the jury (six men instead of the usual twelve because of the scarcity of eligible jurors). The six jury members withdrew to consider their verdict.

Within an hour the jury returned.

"Gentlemen of the jury," asked the judge, "have you reached a verdict?"

"Yes, your honor," the foreman replied, presenting a slip of paper. "We have."

The court stenographer took the paper and handed it to the judge. He read the marks on the paper. His face showed no indication of what he had read, but he looked at the jury with an inquisitive expression. Then he handed the paper back to the stenographer who returned it to the foreman.

Turning his gaze to Star Child who stood dejectedly in the prisoner's box he instructed the prisoner to face the jury. Star Child did so. No doubt he could already feel the rope around his neck.

"The foreman will read the verdict," the judge commanded. "How do you find the defendant?"

The foreman hesitated a moment, looked first around the court then looked at Star Child. He then returned his eyes to the paper.

"We, the jury, find the defendant not guilty."

The spectators erupted. Some gasped angrily—others sat in stunned silence. The police stared in disbelief. Then the little courtroom began to take on the buzz indicative of definite anger. The judge called loudly for order.

With silence restored the judge turned once more to the jury.

"Is your verdict unanimous? So say you all?"

"Yes, your honor," came the reply. "So say we all."

Star Child, still standing, was probably the most surprised man in that little courthouse that afternoon. He stood bewildered not knowing what he should do next. He looked first at the judge, then at the police, then at the notary who had acted as his defense attorney.

"Prisoner, you have been found not guilty and deemed innocent by a jury of your peers," the judge told him, "and so you are, therefore, free to go. The court stands adjourned."

Star Child walked from the court a free man and quickly left town with a couple of friends. The original charge of horse theft was never relaid but, perhaps fearing that it might be remembered once things settled down, he quietly disappeared from Alberta and was heard from no more. In all likelihood he went to Montana once again.

No one in that courtroom could believe the verdict. A review of the evidence, even at this late date, indicates a verdict of guilty was deserved. The jurors defended their decision, citing as their reason great deal of doubt as to the prisoner's guilt. None would go so far as to say they actually believed him to be innocent but they saw the possibility that he might be. The judge himself had instructed them that reasonable doubt demanded a verdict of not guilty. No one believed their explanations and the debate raged in the area for years thereafter.

Why had the jurors disregarded the evidence against Star Child? No one really knows but a possible reason may well have been fear. The jurors were homesteaders living on the prairies some distance from Fort MacLeod, their only immediate protection being their rifles and the stout walls of their sod huts. Did they believe a guilty verdict would have unleashed Indian wrath upon them and their families? Did they fear that each of them would be attacked in a wave of retaliation? That could very well have been their reason.

If that was their fear, it was misplaced. Had Star Child been found guilty, it is unlikely he would have been avenged. The information that had led to his apprehension and arrest had been tipped to the police from within his own village.

Star Child had been given up by his own people.

CHAPTER 18

Last of the Butch Cassidy Gang?

HENRY WAGNER *a.k.a.* Harry Ferguson and The Flying Dutchman
- b. unknown
- d. Nanaimo, B.C., August 28, 1913

Henry Wagner told anybody who would listen that he had been a top lieutenant to Butch Cassidy of The Wild Bunch fame. His claim may have been true, but if it was he had either remained totally anonymous or had ridden with the Wild Bunch under a different name than the two by which he was known to the law. Neither the names Wagner or Ferguson appear at any time in the history of the gang that became known as The Wild Bunch. (Cassidy actually called his gang The Train Robbers' Syndicate but it didn't catch on. The pulp fiction writers renamed them The Hole-in-the-Wall Gang and later they renamed it The Wild Bunch. But that was years after the gang had dispersed forever.)

Neither, so far as is known, was there a Wagner or a Ferguson within the ranks of "Flat Nose" George Currie's gang that preceded that of Cassidy. Wagner stated he had branched out on his own in 1895 when the Cassidy gang was in its final dispersion. If that is true, he covered his tracks very well.

While his origins remain murky, he was very definitely known to lawmen south of the border, his first brush being in 1875. His final experience saw him captured by Canadian lawmen in 1913. It is his in-between years that are shrouded in mystery.

Henry Wagner was representative of the worst kind of Old West badman. He was as vicious and quick to kill as Harry Tracy but lacked Tracy's ability to be polite and sociable if the situation demanded. (Tracy was a member of the Butch Cassidy gang and was a killer of the worst kind.) He was as unpredictable as Jesse James but lacked Jesse's planning ability. He was every bit as elusive as Kid Curry but lacked the kid's daring. He was wanted in at least five western states on murder and robbery charges, was captured several times and always managed to escape. He worked his way west to Colorado (so perhaps he had ridden with Cassidy) then he went north to Montana and finally ended up in Washington State where he robbed post offices.

However, the wild west was so rapidly coming to its end that Wagner found himself an anachronism, an old-time gunslinger in a continent made increasingly smaller through better roads, the telegraph and the newfangled telephone. Stage coaches had long since given way to fast trains that drove the highwaymen out of business. The fast trains ended the days of outlaws such as the Dalton boys by making robbery a risky business. The modern trains were no longer easy to board and, as a couple of enterprising bandits discovered when they got on at a regular stop, traveled too fast to allow safe exit. Those two managed to rob the passengers but were captured at the next stop because couldn't get off. Because of all the changes, Henry Wagner found himself in a world that was evolving faster than he could. Still, he managed to elude American lawmen until 1910 when he ended up in the jail at Walla Walla, Washington, with a long sentence for robbing a bank. Always industrious, he managed to escape one night in 1912.

He and a cowardly, small-time crook named Bill Julian had teamed up in prison. When Wagner told Julian of his intent to escape, the latter happily agreed to help him. The mismatched pair managed a clean break, but following the break they needed money in order to stay on the run. Wagner, reverting to normal, decided a post office would be an easy target, as post offices always kept money on the premises and were usually staffed with a minimum of workers. The pair first broke into a hardware store where they stole some guns and ammunition. Then they lit out on the road to freedom traveling through the heavy forest toward the coast.

Wagner chose as his target the post office in a small wayside town and the pair burst in waving their guns shouting "This is a hold up! Everyone stay still." A small amount of cash was scooped from the drawer but then things began to go wrong. Either a customer or the postmaster produced a pistol and commenced firing. Julian, a frightened man at the best of times, ran from the building but Wagner traded shots as he backed out the door, killing the postmaster in the exchange. He and Julian, wealthier by far less than they had anticipated, headed once again into the woods. From there they kept going west toward the Puget Sound area.

Knowing they had run out of American corners in which to hide (and possibly mindful of the relentless pursuit and killing of Harry Tracy in 1902 by a combined Washington and Oregon posse) they avoided all settlements. Arriving at Tacoma, a coast port, they stole a motor yacht—a sturdy, seaworthy craft called *Spray*. The boat was powered by a gasoline engine and had full tanks. Julian would likely have passed right by but Wagner had been thinking, so when he saw the *Spray* he made a decision on the spot. They would, he informed the bewildered Julian, escape to Canada.

The fugitives clambered aboard, started the motor and cast off into the stream, Wagner at the helm and Julian at the engine. He pointed the bow northward and headed up the sound.

Wagner had decided that Canada would provide the refuge he craved. Whether he knew anything about Canada is unknown but it is not beyond the realm of imagination that he thought of it as a vast hinterland of tall trees and no population. On the other hand he may have known something about the land because he steered unerringly for Vancouver Island.

Hugging the coastline and sailing between the numerous islands that dot those southwest waters he avoided Victoria as he navigated northward. Whether he had a destination in mind is unknown but when he eventually spotted Lasqueti Island, a large island at the time uninhabited; he knew that it would be a suitable hideaway. He found a narrow inlet and eased the boat into the quiet waters.

Lasqueti lies six miles off the shore of Vancouver Island midway between Qualicum Bay and Texada Island. That it was the perfect place to hide makes it seem feasible that Wagner actually knew something about Canada's western coast. Perhaps his murky past included origins north of the border. Perhaps he had been born and raised in Canada. No one can say with certainty.

Wagner and Julian found a sheltered indentation in the little sound, hid the boat and went ashore. They built a small cabin and settled to the task of making the island their hideout. They could have lived there undetected for months—perhaps years—had they minded their own business, kept a low profile and lived off the land.

The island abounded in animals, birds and edible vegetation. However, their business was thievery, so it lay beyond the resolution of either to settle into a life of gathering birds' eggs and eating herbs to complement their deer steaks. Within a couple of weeks the two grew restless. An uninhabited island is, after all, not everyone's cup of tea, herbal or otherwise.

One evening, while sitting in the slowly descending darkness watching lights flickering across the water on the big island, Wagner had an idea. He called Julian to explain his plan.

"Bill, old horse," he announced, "we are going to visit those little towns that are strung along the coast and gather enough loot to finance our return to the States and a new life."

"What about the cops?" asked Julian. "There sure as hell are police over there."

"What would a bunch of yokels up here know about being lawmen?" Wagner snarled. "I am not afraid of a bunch of policemen who wear fancy uniforms. Don't you know I once faced down three U.S. marshals all carrying shotguns? I didn't ride with Butch Cassidy just to keep him company, y'know. These guys up here don't scare me."

Julian may have had his doubts about the claim but he was not inclined to argue with Henry Wagner. He had seen him with a six-gun and knew he wasn't afraid to use it.

Henry Wagner, never one to stay still once an idea had come to mind, formulated a plan of attack. He would avoid the big centers, such as Courtenay to the north and Nanaimo sixty miles (106 km) to the south. No need to risk big towns, there were plenty of small ones to visit. Whether Julian had any input to his scheme is unknown, but Julian was a cringing man who would go along with anyone tougher than he so probably he remained silent on the issue.

Wagner soon put his plans into effect. Using the *Spray* to travel back and forth to the big island he and his partner hit a different town every time, deliberately keeping their hits separated by many miles. He reasoned, quite correctly, that the first robberies would be considered random and that no one would think for one minute that the same gang was responsible for all. Fuel for the boat proved no problem either. Fuel was simply stolen from moored boats targeted along the way to the selected town. It was an easy matter to ease alongside an empty fishing boat, locate the tank filler and siphon fuel into the *Spray*. Besides, the *Spray* had two large tanks and did not need refilling often.

Thus, began one of the strangest crime waves in the history of Vancouver Island. Such was its scope that it cannot be considered surprising the authorities thought a large gang was involved. The two-man "gang" eventually hit every settlement, village and town between Nanaimo and Courtenay. They at first followed the original plan closely in that they limited their enterprise to break and enter burglaries carried out randomly with several nights between. Rarely were more than two stores entered in each robbery. If the town had a post office, it was always on the list for whatever cash it might contain. The usual targets were general stores, hardware and grocery stores with loot ranging from rifles to portable machinery to groceries. All the missing items were either usable or easily sold and that at first caused local police officers to think the robbers were local criminals.

The first suspects naturally were those who were "known to police," but all enquiries came up empty. Likewise, there was nothing turning up in the storerooms of those known to be "receivers of stolen goods." The frustrations grew and grew as leads appeared only to be discarded one by one.

Investigators knew the amount of loot being taken could never be removed without a reasonably sized conveyance. They also felt that several individuals had to be involved as one man would be hard-pressed to handle all that was being taken. The thieves, investigators reasoned, had to have a horse-drawn wagon. With that in mind investigators concentrated their efforts to tracking along trails and side roads. Nothing materialized. Experienced trackers continuously came up empty until it seemed the thieves, their horse and their wagon were simply vanishing into thin air following each raid.

At first Wagner and Julian were content to raid one town per night but soon greed overtook Henry. He realized he had mobility with the *Spray* and decided to raid two towns in a single night. It would be an easy matter to leave one town with the loot it had afforded then steer for another a few miles distant. Each town would be a fair journey by road in those days when automobiles were nonexistent except in certain big cities, but distance posed no problem for a boat like the *Spray*. That idea, good as it was, proved his ultimate undoing for it quickly showed the emergence of a definite pattern, one easy to gauge.

When Wagner decided that if one night was good two had to be better he increased not only his area but his loot. However, when he again broadened his scope by raiding two towns on two consecutive nights he gave investigating police officers a valuable clue. To that point each officer had been treating each burglary as a local situation. Following several of these multiple break-ins a pattern began to emerge, a pattern that showed the thieves to be remarkably mobile. The police began sharing information on a more regular basis.

Then, when Wagner went into robberies at distance, the police knew that a special mobility was involved. Again their thoughts naturally turned to a wagon; but without leaving a single track or hoof mark, how was it being done? Not only was it impossible for thieves with a horse and wagon to leave no trail, it was equally impossible to stage burglaries in two towns separated by many miles using a plodding horse-drawn wagon. They began to look at other possibilities, including a theory of a split gang. No one had considered the thieves might be using a boat.

Meanwhile, the exploits of the as yet unidentified Wagner began to tweak the imagination of the public and the press. A reporter began to compare the elusive burglar to the lead character in Richard Wagner's mythic opera *The Flying Dutchman*—obviously present yet never seen. The name caught on. The general public—and even the police—began to refer to the mysterious thief by that name. That Henry shared a surname with Richard was just one of fate's classic jokes. The two were not in all likelihood even remotely related.

The Flying Dutchman, elusive as ever, continued his hit and run tactics over the next several months. But he was running out of time. His luck deserted him in Union Bay, a coastal village some fifty miles north of Nanaimo and ten miles south of Courtenay. He had been betrayed by his greed and his failure to avoid following set paths. Henry Wagner had become a creature of habit. His inability to change set patterns did him in.

For weeks a team of investigators working from a room in Nanaimo followed the string of burglaries as they extended down the island. Following each report, a mark was made on a map until a definite pattern began to emerge. It soon showed that repeat calls were always being made on post offices but not always on private stores. Obviously the Flying Dutchman was in need of cash. To the investigators this meant he was hoping to gain money probably in order to change location with a minimum of bother.

So far none of his loot had shown up. Did this mean, they wondered, that he was preparing to leave with his ill-gotten booty and sell it all to one buyer? It seemed reasonable to assume he would need a large amount of money in order to transport the goods from the area. If this was the case, he would continue to rob the post offices. They decided to concentrate on those positioned along the road between Nanaimo and Courtenay.

The markers showed the investigators the Flying Dutchman was a creature of habit. The last post office robbed was close to Nanaimo but they felt he was not likely to try anything as risky as a foray into Vancouver Island's second largest community. Neither had he burglarized any stores in Courtenay, the third largest. He was smart enough to concentrate on small, sparsely policed settlements. According to the message showing in the line of markers, providing the Flying Dutchman continued along a set path, the post office at Union Bay was due to be hit once again—and very soon. All concentration, reason told them, should be set upon that small village.

About April 29, 1913, two B.C. Police constables, Gordon Ross and Harry Westaway, were called to the office of the district superintendent of B.C. Police at his Nanaimo headquarters. Westaway was a rookie officer who showed great promise; Ross had been with the force for some time and had earned a great deal of respect for his investigative capabilities. The two were briefed in full on the progress of the Flying Dutchman case and given explicit orders.

"You are to go to Union Bay," the superintendent told them. "Wear clothing that will make you look as if you are laborers in search of casual work. Make inquiries about local work but pretend interest in the coal mines at Cumberland should anyone ask. Stay in the town, but lie as low as possible because you mustn't draw attention to yourselves in any way. Above all, do not have any dealings with the town constable. He will want to help and this is something you have to do on your own.

"When you arrive go to the post office and see the postmaster. He is expecting you and will give you a key to his building. At night hide inside somewhere where you can watch both doors. If the Dutchman and his friends break in you must do what you must do. Take him alive if possible but...."

The superintendent shrugged his shoulders letting the unfinished sentence speak for itself.

"Does the constable know we are coming?" Ross asked.

"No. Only the postmaster knows," the superintendent replied. "No one else must know because this gang might have informants, although I rather doubt that."

"Very well, sir," Ross replied. "Harry and I will be able to blend in with the population without trouble. There are a lot of itinerant coal miners coming and going to Cumberland so a couple more won't be noticed."

"Just be careful and stay on your toes," the superintendent said. "We don't know a damn thing about this so-called Flying Dutchman, what he looks like or who he might be. He could be anyone."

The men talked a while longer exchanging points of view. Westaway wondered if any wanted posters on current fugitives might give a clue or two and a few were looked at but no ideas were forthcoming. Shortly thereafter Ross and Westaway took their leave, went to their respective homes to outfit themselves with workers' clothes. The next morning they each packed a small bag into which they placed their pistols, pinned their police badges and identification cards safely inside their shirts and caught the morning stage to Union Bay, a trip which took the better part of the day.

Upon arrival Westaway checked himself and Ross into the local hotel while his partner called on the postmaster to collect the key. Ross knew the job could last many days—or it might end that night. They could sleep all day if need be, for if anything was going to happen it would occur during the dark hours. The really difficult part of the operation would be to allay any suspicious glances from the town constable. That worthy might not like the idea of two strangers hanging around his town too long and could easily cause troubles for the pair of undercover officers.

For three nights Ross and Westaway stood watch in the building that housed the post office. Union Bay was a small village so they were also well positioned to hear any unusual happening that might occur in any of the adjoining structures. Each night the two let themselves in quietly after darkness had engulfed the town and each morning just before dawn they let themselves out just as quietly. They would then sneak back to the hotel, creep to their room for a few hours sleep, then make an appearance about noon. It was necessary to keep up the illusion of two men seeking employment. If they slept all day, it would cause raised eyebrows of which two might belong to the town constable.

During the evening of May 4, Wagner and Julian started the *Spray*'s engine, turned her bow westward and steered WNW, a course for Union Bay, some ninety miles distant. Wagner had decided to begin his next southern swing by hitting the post office there for the second time. The *Spray* could manage the run in a little more than two hours but Wagner, wanting as quiet a run as possible, would throttle down as he neared Denman Island. Thus, the run would take closer to three hours but time was not important. There was no use arriving until after midnight.

The trip went well. Wagner had made the run several times now and with Julian keeping a watchful eye in front obstacles could be easily avoided. If anyone should hear the boat's engine he, unable to see it, would lose interest quickly. The greatest danger was from floating logs but Julian would see such a hazard in plenty of time. The Flying Dutchman had every reason to feel secure.

Arriving near Union Bay shortly after midnight, the two anchored the *Spray* inside a secluded inlet about a half mile from the village. Using a small boat the two rowed to shore, pulled the boat onto the beach then scurried through the bush for the village. Skirting from building to building they came to the post office's rear door without incidence. Using a metal bar with a flattened end, Wagner forced the door open. The only sound was a single, sharp "clunk!" as the lock wrenched loose from the door jamb. He quietly pushed the door open. He, with Julian right behind, slipped into the darkened room.

Ross and Westaway had listened as the door was wrenched open. They had positioned themselves to afford the most opportune vision of all sides. They had also made one serious mistake. Both officers had left their pistols snug within their holsters. This was a failing in many Canadian lawmen. Perhaps this fault was due to the fact that so many were of British background and felt the authority of the law was enough to subdue a criminal. Unfortunately, most outlaws held no such feelings toward the law.

When Wagner and Julian entered the building, Ross allowed them to gain a few feet of entry then, identifying himself as an officer of the B.C. Police, he called to them to surrender. Wagner, who had his .45 Colt already drawn, turned toward the voice and fired one shot. But, because he could not see in the near pitch dark, he fired blindly. The shot, though it missed Ross, hit Westaway squarely in the chest. The rookie officer staggered out into the night, mortally wounded. Julian also turned and ran, leaving Wagner to face the trouble alone.

Ross, surprised by the shot, did not have time to draw his pistol. But his eyes were accustomed to the darkness and, as he could see Wagner, he hurled himself against the man wrapping his powerful arms around him to prevent the pistol being used again. A very large, powerful man, Ross grappled with the outlaw and, following a bitter rough and tumble fight during which Wagner dropped the pistol, Ross clubbed him into unconsciousness with his fists and the billy club he had managed to unhook from Wagner's belt.

Meanwhile, the gunshot and ensuing noise had attracted the town's constable who came running, gun drawn. Ross, still clubbing Wagner, hauled the struggling man outside to the wooden sidewalk saw the constable and shouted for him to handcuff the struggling Wagner. The constable, having no idea of who was whom, hesitated forcing Ross to shout that he was a police officer. The constable decided that was sufficient identification for him and he cuffed the bloodied and battered Wagner, who, when Ross released his grip, fell unconscious to the ground. Ross dragged his prisoner to a nearby pole and, using his own cuffs, secured Wagner's hands around it to make certain he could not get away.

Meanwhile, a doctor was called to attend to Westaway. Unfortunately, the officer died shortly after. The doctor then treated Ross for bites and other cuts. Wagner was eventually treated for his injuries but not for some time as Westaway and Ross were considered priorities. Besides, Wagner was still unconscious and remained so for some time.

Once treated, Wagner was taken, heavily chained, to the police station. He was soon identified from Washington wanted posters, confessed all and told Ross the identity of his cohort who had escaped, but he refused to reveal the location of the hideout. Likely he was harboring plans to escape. Wagner was locked up securely to await transfer to Nanaimo and the hunt for Bill Julian began.

Julian enjoyed a limited freedom. He had, in his cowardly manner, run from the post office to where the *Spray* was anchored. He rowed the small boat to the yacht, hauled it inboard, got the engine started and made for Lasqueti Island at top speed. There he stayed until he was found less than two weeks later. A coastal patrolman spotted a man matching Julian's description rowing a small boat in one of Lasqueti Island's inlets. He easily arrested the weary Julian.

Julian was taken to Nanaimo where he gave the police the information they wanted including directions to the cabin he and Wagner had built on the island. A search of the cabin uncovered all the loot from the break-ins, excepting the liquor and food the two had consumed.

Charged with the murder of a police officer, the pair broke all records trying to blame the other. Ross felt certain that Wagner had fired the fatal shot and concentrated his attentions on the cringing Julian. To assure his cooperation he was made an offer he could not refuse: testify against Wagner, the authorities promised, and he would not hang. He would also be protected from his erstwhile partner. Julian feared Wagner more than he dreaded the hangman. At the guarantee of protection, however, he agreed to the terms.

The trial was short for the evidence was overwhelming. When Julian took the stand the case was sealed. Julian made an excellent witness for he recounted in detail the pair's escapades from the time they broke out of the Walla Walla penitentiary to the minute Wagner fired his pistol in Union Bay.

The jury had no trouble arriving at a verdict. Wagner and Julian were both found guilty of murder. Wagner was sentenced to hang while Julian was given what seemed to many as an extremely lenient five years as an accomplice. The sentence was not all that lenient for when he was eventually released from the penitentiary at New Westminster he was immediately thrust into the waiting arms of a Washington marshal who took him south to stand trial on an assortment of charges, several of which carried the death penalty.

Wagner did not await his death date with noticeable courage. He spent his first two weeks in his cell telling all and sundry how he had ridden with Butch Cassidy back in the 1890s and bragging that he would escape with his first order of business being that of killing Bill Julian.

When it became obvious, even to him, that escape was impossible he withdrew into silence. As his time drew nearer, he tried to kill himself by repeatedly banging his head against the cell wall. His efforts proved unsuccessful but he did manage to severely injure his brain. He began to suffer epileptic-like seizures and, in fact, had just regained consciousness from one when the guards arrived to take him to his date with Mr. Radcliffe, the hangman. (An alias was used by hangmen to assure anonymity. A fellow called Mr. Ellis succeeded Mr. Radcliffe and was Canada's last hangman.)

However, when Wagner came into sight of the gallows his old bravado reemerged. He straightened up, shook off the restraining hands of the guards, walked crisply to the steps, bounded up the steps two at a time then stood patiently while a black hood was placed over his head and the noose secured around his neck. He said something to the hangman (those last words were never revealed) then nodded that he was ready. The hangman pulled the lever and the trap dropped open.

Henry Wagner, alias Harry Ferguson, possibly one of Butch Cassidy's trusted lieutenants, whose elusiveness had earned him the soubriquet "The Flying Dutchman" plunged into eternity early on the morning of August 28, 1913.

Constable Gordon Ross remained in the B.C. Police building an impressive record for several more years. He was eventually offered, and accepted, the position of Chief of Police for the city of Vancouver. He held that position for many years adding to his credits and then enjoyed several more years of quiet retirement.

CHAPTER 19

Deadly Delinquents—
The McLean Gang

- Allan (1854 to Jan. 31, 1881)
- Charlie (1862 to Jan. 31, 1881)
- Archie (1864 to Jan. 31, 1881)
- Alex Hare (1862 to Jan. 31, 1881)

During the years 1878 to1880 a wide area around Kamloops, B.C., was terrorized by a gang of three brothers and their cousin. Rampaging without apparent pattern, the gang struck here and there with wild abandon. What made them doubly dangerous was the gang's range. Being expert horsemen, all four were able to ride long distances in a short time. Worse, the attacks were random indicating the members had no specific grievances against any persons or institutions in particular—they hated everyone.

Unlike outlaws such as Jesse James or Bill Miner who vented their rages and hatreds against banks and railroads the McLean boys attacked anything that took their fancy. No one was safe but for some reason they treated women kindly. They intimidated them but never moved to cause harm to them.

Allan, the oldest at age twenty-five, was the leader. Charlie was but seventeen when they started their last rampage. The youngest brother, Archie, was only fourteen. The fourth member of this murderous quartet was a cousin, Alex Hare. Little is known of Hare except that he was only a few days older than Charlie and had been a bosom buddy to the two youngest McLeans.

The brothers McLean were the sons of Donald McLean, who was murdered in 1864, shot in the back by an unknown assailant (possibly one of his own men) while fighting in the Chilcotin

Uprising. The boys' mother was the second of his two Native wives. (The Chilcotin Uprising occurred in 1864 when a group of Chilcotin Indians, angered by the encroachment of whites into their lands, killed several trappers and settlers. A war of sorts waged for several months until the Natives surrendered. Three chiefs were hanged in 1866 for the original murders.)

Donald McLean, an ill-tempered, hard-drinking, brutal Scotsman, was totally devoid of compassion or social graces. He trapped for the Hudson's Bay Company throughout the Thompson and Nicola Valleys. Although he married two Indian women, McLean despised all Indians and had absolutely nothing but loathing for children of mixed parentage. This, despite the fact that his own eleven children fell into that category. His attitude toward Indians is emphasized in an incident that occurred about 1849. An HBC employee had been killed by an Indian and McLean joined the posse that ran him down. Although the posse cornered the man and had him where an arrest could have been made, McLean shot the fugitive. Then he also shot down the man's son-in-law, an uncle and an infant who happened to be in the cabin in which the fugitive was hiding. Indians later made several attempts to avenge those senseless killings but Donald McLean survived—until he was back-shot.

Charlie and Allan were probably doomed from their very beginnings because of the physical abuses received at the hands of their violent father. Archie, born just weeks before Donald was killed, never knew his vicious sire but was little better off because of the abject poverty he knew in his life with his mother. Why fate singled out the three boys is open to conjecture because their eight half-siblings seem to have fared much better.

It was the McLean boys' misfortune that they possessed no Indian features. Had they resembled the Native people they would have been accepted by them, but all three boys were blond and blue-eyed. The Indians shunned them as "white"; but because they were half Indian, there was no place for them in white society at the time. Thus, they grew up in the bigoted world of two societies neither of which was willing to compromise.

Indeed, at their trial their defense attorney pleaded the boys' cases, with no success whatever, on the grounds of their unhappy upbringing and their shattered dreams of acceptance into either of the two societies. Today such a defense would have received a great deal of consideration.

Allan, Charlie and Archie were outlaws from their earliest years—Archie had officially been declared an outlaw at age eleven, but the lawmen in the area never bothered exercising the edict because his exploits were deemed the works of a bad boy rather than those of a bad man. He was never arrested. Overall, Archie was without doubt the worst of the three. He fits the classic description of a psychopathic killer.

Charlie, on the other hand, was arrested once. When he was fifteen, he attacked another youth and, during the grappling that ensued, bit off the tip of his opponent's nose. The police now had no choice but to charge him with aggravated assault for which he received a jail term of three months. Taken to the jail in Kamloops, he stayed all of three days before escaping. No one bothered looking for him.

Allan would probably have turned out all right had it not been for the federal and B.C. governments' tight-fisted policies governing Indians. Ottawa had set aside lands for Indians but refused the same provisions for "half-breeds." Neither were they allowed to be enrolled in schools. As a result Allan received no education, no land grants and no other assistance. However, he did marry and fathered one child but was rarely at home to help raise him. His father-in-law was Chillinetza, the chief of the Nicola tribe. Ironically, Chillinetza would be a member of the posse that eventually ran the McLean gang to ground.

Until the McLeans turned to robbery and murder, the boys worked as cowhands at some of the local ranches. They were good workers, could rope and brand a calf in record time, knew the ins and outs of trail drives and got along with their fellow drovers. They spent most of their spare time drinking and fighting in the local towns but outside of paying small fines when charged with being drunk and disorderly never found themselves in serious trouble. They were all expert riders and crack shots with rifles and pistols.

During the winter months, when ranches traditionally cut their staffs to a few permanent riders, the McLeans earned money cutting trees for firewood and shooting deer for meat. They also stole a lot of their food by various means. They stole from everyone—Indian, white, poor and rich alike. They ranged from the northern reaches of the Thompson Valley to the southern border, raided into Washington Territory to rustle horses and cattle. They looted ranch houses and stores, taking blankets, guns, ammunition and harness equipment. When they robbed ranch houses, they cleaned out the liquor cabinets as well as the food cupboards. During the winter of 1877 they decided that pillage and plunder beat low wages and long hours. Outlawry became their full-time occupation.

In 1878, now steadily accompanied by Alex Hare, they went on a personal warpath. Although they eluded the law for less than two years until they were caught, they rode rampant across the land, burning, pillaging, robbing banks, plundering houses and murdering anyone who got in the way. They used their vast knowledge of the hills and valleys to move unseen between hideouts. And when a posse did manage to encounter them, the boys used their great riding skills to outride the pursuers. When it came to gunplay, their marksmanship easily drove the posse members into cover. By the time they worked up the courage to emerge, the McLeans and Hare would be gone—seemingly vanished once again into thin air.

As the months wore on, the gang's excesses became more and more vicious. During their final months the gang went from one outrage to another. They especially targeted a Kamloop's merchant, John O'Mara, who had taken the McLean's sister Annie as his mistress. They sent word to Kamloops that O'Mara would be killed and that the town would be put to the torch in atonement for that sin. That threat (never carried out) was enough to throw panic into the townspeople. Appeals to the B.C. government to increase the one-man police force fell on deaf ears. Fear of the McLeans pushed Kamloops' citizens into a sort of siege mentality.

Learning of the town's request to Victoria the gang laid low for a while. Then, when the government denied the plea, the gang's sense of invincibility increased. The four went on a tear. In 1879, a very cold December, they stole a prized stallion from the paddock of William Palmer, a prominent rancher. It was a mistake, for Palmer was hardly a man to trifle with. He tracked the gang to their hideout. There he found the three McLeans drunk. They were also waving rifles and pistols but he took a chance anyway and rode into the camp. Perhaps the boys were surprised that a white man should show that type of naive courage and they invited him to sit a spell and warm himself by the fire.

Wisely, Palmer decided just to talk to the boys without mentioning the horse. After a few words he made his goodbyes, walked out of the camp to his mount, turned and rode away. He knew without doubt that Archie was itching for an excuse to shoot him so he had kept his hand well away from his gun butt.

Palmer rode directly to Kamloops where he swore out a complaint against the gang for horse theft. With a warrant in hand he and John Ussher, the town constable, rode to the camp in company with a tracker and another rancher.

The small posse found the McLeans and Hare still camped where Palmer had left them. As the riders approached, one of the gang fired. The bullet singed Palmer's whiskers and hit John McLeod, the rancher. Palmer returned fire which brought on a fusillade from the gang. McLeod was hit in the leg and his horse was hit several times. Ussher called out to the gang that they must surrender.

Allan indicated they were willing to talk so Ussher dismounted, left his rifle with Palmer and walked slowly toward the camp, hands forward with palms up. He was close to the gang when suddenly Alex Hare leapt from a bush and began stabbing Ussher with a Bowie knife. Then Archie McLean ran up, rifle in hand, and shot the helpless lawman in the head killing him instantly.

The remaining three possemen, realizing Ussher was dead, retreated at full gallop for Kamloops. There McLeod was treated for his several wounds, none of which proved too serious. Then a larger posse was assembled and headed out to the scene of the ambush. Ussher's body, frozen solid, was found stripped of his clothing and boots. The gang was gone but there was evidence that at least one had been wounded. As things turned out, the wounded man was Charlie; but his wounds, though painful, were not serious.

The McLeans and Hare fled toward the Douglas Lake Indian Reserve. Along the way they killed James Kelly, a sheepherder against whom they held a grudge. Kelly had laid a complaint against them for stealing some of his sheep as well as brandy and bread. They looted his tiny cabin of food and took a pistol and ammunition as well.

A short distance away was the ranch owned by Tom Trapp, so they rode there and informed the frightened Trapp that they had killed Kelly. Then they took Trapp's rifle plus a pistol and several boxes of ammunition. Archie wanted to kill Trapp but Allan talked him out of it much to Trapp's relief. However, the matter was not settled without the toss of a coin. Archie called "heads" and Allan won when the coin showed "tails." The gang left Trapp standing at his cabin door and galloped away into the bush.

Their next stop was at a farm owned by John Roberts. They came upon Roberts with drawn pistols and told him to sit down as they had something to tell him. They spent quite some time waving the guns while they regaled Roberts with the details of how they had killed Ussher and Kelly. They then told him to spread the word that the gang intended to kill Palmer, McLeod and several others. They asked Roberts for information about others, white men and Indians with whom they professed to have unfinished business. Roberts replied he knew nothing of the people mentioned so the gang left. Even the maniacal Archie made no move to harm the farmer.

Before they actually arrived at the Douglas Lake Reserve, however, the gang made one last stop—at the Palmer ranch. Palmer was not home but his wife was there. Nonetheless, the gang members treated her with great civility and politeness. Allan informed her that she should tell her husband that he should convince the posse to stop the search for the four outlaws.

"If the lawmen follow us," Allan told her, "we will kill them all including Palmer."

"I—I will tell them what you said," Mrs. Palmer promised.

"Good," said Allan. "Now we will drink Palmer's brandy and then take his guns and bullets."

While Mrs. Palmer sat trembling in a corner, the gang spent the next hour pouring liberal helpings of brandy into glasses and slugging back the fiery liquor. They swept through the house in search of weapons and ammunition. Finally, they mounted their mustangs and rode away toward the reserve.

When they arrived at the reserve, they attempted to incite the Indians into revolting against the whites but the memory of the Chilcotin Uprising disaster was too fresh in the Indians' memories and they refused to listen. Allan then went to Chief Chillinetza.

"Join with us, father-in-law," he implored the elderly man, "and we will rise against the white men. Your warriors are many and our tribe is strong. We have many rifles. Join with us."

"You would cause our people to go into a war we cannot win," the chief replied. "No one will follow you along a war trail that is of such folly."

"The whites have cheated our people," countered Allan McLean. "They have taken the good land and left our people with soil that grows nothing. They have given lands on which grow only scrubby trees. And to men like myself they have offered nothing."

If he had really held a hope that the Nicola people would follow him and his outlaw brothers into a full scale rebellion his hope was quickly dashed.

"No, my son-in-law," Chillinetza replied, "I will not allow my people to follow you into certain death. True, the whites have treated us badly but they have not killed us. I ask you to change your path. Stay with us, return to your wife, my daughter, and to your son, my grandchild. Give up your ways for you ride only to death."

Once again Allan swept his arm across the formidable arsenal of rifles and pistols his gang had amassed. His gesture indicated there were plenty of fire arms for what he had in mind. But the old chief slowly shook his head.

"I say once again, son-in-law, the answer is no. If you will not stay here and change your life then you must go," the chief replied. "It is best if you ride quickly to the southern lands below the medicine line. Join our cousins, the Walla Walla or the Wenatchee. They will give you refuge and tend to your needs."

"You are ordering me to leave this place?" asked Allan.

"I am saying only that to stay here will place you and your brothers in the gravest danger," Chillinetza replied, sadly. "The lawmen will come here for certain. They will surely find you."

"Charlie is wounded," Allan said. "There is an abandoned cabin on the shore of Douglas Lake. Will you stop us from using it until he well enough to travel?"

"I will not stop you," replied the chief, "but I must tell you your friends here are very few. There are rewards for your capture. You should be careful because there are those among the Nicola who would betray you to the lawmen. The money will tempt many."

The McLeans and Hare rode silently out of the reserve watched by a number of Indians. None offered to join them and this must have disappointed the outlaws. They had thought they would be welcomed, that their rifles would convince many to join them. It was not to be.

One Indian watched the four with special interest. As they rode out of sight he followed on foot, shadowing the group as they picked their way through the scrubby trees. Following was easy; the horses could not move quickly through the bush. The Indian watched from a safe distance as the gang approached a deserted cabin, dismounted and prepared to settle in. Then he ran back to the village where he mounted his horse and rode at full gallop toward Kamloops.

The cabin was cold but had a place to build a small fire. Charlie was helped inside and made as comfortable as possible. His wounds, though not life-threatening, were painful and his limbs had begun to stiffen because of poor blood circulation. The first order of business was to restore warmth to his chilled body. A fire was started and soon the tiny cabin was snugly warm. Archie cooked some of the food the gang had stolen from Walker's house, made sure his brother ate a fair share then watched as Charlie fell into a sound sleep. He would feel much better in the morning.

Meanwhile, the Indian who had followed the gang arrived at Kamloops. He went directly to the police office and asked to speak with the chief officer. He was ushered into the presence of Constable George Caughill who asked what he wanted.

"Is a reward offered for the McLeans and Alex Hare?" the Indian asked.

Caughill affirmed an offer was on the books for the capture of the four men.

"I know where they camp," the Indian said.

"Will you lead us there?" asked the constable.

"How much I get?" the Indian asked.

"Fifty dollars," Caughill replied.

"One hundred dollars," the Indian countered.

"It's a deal," replied Caughill.

"When I get money?" the Indian wanted to know.

"When we catch them, the money will be paid," Caughill promised.

"Good," came the reply, "but no one know."

"No one will know," the constable said. "But how will you explain that kind of money to others?"

"Many furs this year," the Indian retorted. "Traps have good magic this year."

With the negotiations finished Caughill bade the informant to stay handy while he sent word to the magistrate in Nicola, the county seat. Within a few hours a reply message informed him that John Clapperton, the district justice of the peace, had authorized the reward be paid.

A few hours later armed men in several groups moved slowly into position around the lonely cabin. A message was sent to New

Westminster informing the government that a large posse had surrounded the cabin in which the gang was holed up. Throughout the Thompson Valley the word spread. Missionaries were quick to tell their congregations that the McLean issue was not one of the Indians. Tribal chiefs told their people not to become involved. The McLeans had brought their troubles upon themselves. There was no reason for Indians to help them.

It was at this point the McLeans, had they been able to make themselves present, would have found out just how many friends they had among their people. The answer was very, very few. Their excesses had been too severe. Even the few friends they had within the Indian community (they had none among the whites) opted to have nothing more to do with them. In fact, the posse was augmented by many Indians, including Chief Chillinetza, and a large number of half-breeds.

On December 09, 1879, the four awakened to find themselves trapped in their cabin. Looking out the tiny openings in the cabin wall they could see only armed men. They had to know at that point there was no chance of escape. They would have to fight it out. Quickly taking stock of what they had at hand they realized they had enough guns and ammunition to stand off an army. They also had enough food to last throughout a very long siege. They must have been shattered, though, to find there was no water. The one thing they had not laid in store was the one thing they needed more than anything else. Throughout the entire siege the only water the gang could get was from the snow they managed to scrape from the chinks in the walls. It was not nearly enough.

John Chillerton, the magistrate from Nicola, called on the four to surrender. He was answered by a barrage of gunfire. The posse settled down to wait. There was no hurry. By now they had seen the sticks and hands emerging from time to time through the holes in the walls scratching for snow. That told them their quarry had no water. They would wait.

Wait they did. One, two, three days slid by in cold monotony broken only by an occasional volley of gunfire. On the third day a sort of negotiation began. Indian messengers were recruited to take messages into the fugitives. Some were written as it was learned that Alex Hare was able to read. The replies were all verbal, though. Alex, apparently, was unable to write. Eventually, all the messages became verbal.

The messages had no results, but the lack of water was beginning to take a toll on the four. Late on the third day they made a break for an outbuilding where their horses had been tethered. The animals, however, had long since been taken by the posse under cover of darkness. The four ran directly into a wall of fire and quickly retreated trading shots as they ran. Three of the posse were wounded.

Waiting is always tedious, especially in frigid temperatures, so the posse members decided to end the siege. On December 13, a Friday, a wagon was loaded with hay and straw, doused with kerosene, set ablaze and pushed toward the cabin. The plan failed. Fifty feet short of the cabin those pushing the wagon were met with a hail of bullets and another posseman fell wounded. The outlaws made great cheers to celebrate this minor victory. It was their last hurrah.

Inside the cabin conditions had become untenable. The small room was smoky, the smell of human waste was becoming unbearable and the outlaws were so thirsty they were having trouble thinking straight. Whether they voted on it is unknown but one by one the four emerged from the cabin, hands held high. The siege was over. The posse moved in, handcuffed the four and the police officers informed the four that, formally, they were under arrest.

Trussed securely hand and foot they were transported first to Kamloops then to New Westminster by canoe, raft and stagecoach. The journey took several days but on December 25, they were ensconced in the jail at New Westminster.

During their stay the four caused their jailers more trouble than would have dozens of prisoners. All four ended up in solitary confinement. All four received beatings as well. This charge was investigated and several guards were reprimanded, albeit not severely, because of the trouble the four had caused.

The trial of the McLean Gang began under heavy security in March, 1880. The defense presented the best arguments possible but their arguments were 100 years too early. In 1880 juries were not interested in considering the woes of underprivileged childhoods, drunken fathers and a society that shunned those who were different. Archie and Charlie did not help their cause in the least by the behavior they displayed. If there was any sympathy shown, it would have been for Allan.

The jury retired for deliberation and were out for some time. The twelve men might have returned a guilty verdict with a recommendation for mercy had it not been for the brutal murder of Constable Ussher, who had gone to parley, unarmed, in peace. The killing of sheepherder Kelly also bothered them because Kelly had given up his weapons without argument. The jury returned a guilty verdict and made no recommendation for mercy.

With such a verdict the judge quietly intoned the sentence: death by hanging. He set the date for January 31, 1881. As the four were being led from the courtroom they fought with their guards and tried to scramble across the railing to get at Walker, their old nemesis.

Over the next nine months the usual appeals worked their ways through the court system to be heard in various higher courts. Each appeal in turn was denied until the case reached the Supreme Court. That court found the trial judge had erred in points of law and ordered a new trial.

The McLean Gang's second trial was heard in November with the same charges, the same lawyers, the same evidence, the same witnesses but with a different judge and, of course, a different jury. The verdict was the same: guilty as charged. As in the first trial, there was no recommendation for mercy. The judge pronounced the same sentence with the same date as that of the original judge.

The second trial took the fight out of the four. From that day forward none, even the psychopathic Archie, gave any further trouble. They cooperated with their jailers, accepted the ministrations of the prison chaplains and appeared resigned to their fates.

On the final day of their lives the four outlaws walked bravely to the scaffold. There were no tears or shows of emotion or signs of fight. Only Archie showed a degree of defiance. When asked if he had any last words he simply said that he didn't care if he was hanged and didn't care if everyone knew it. He owed nothing to no one. Then the four walked together up the thirteen wooden steps and stood together on the trapdoor where they listened in silence to the final prayer of the chaplain.

Shortly after 8:00 a.m. the trap fell out from under their feet. Thirty minutes later each was pronounced dead and were cut down.

Archie had just turned sixteen, but looked no more than thirteen. Alex Hare and Charlie were just seventeen. Allan was twenty-seven.

The hanging of the McLeans marks the one time in Canadian history that three brothers have been hanged on the same gallows at the same time.

CHAPTER 20

The Two-Fisted Town Tamer

JOHN S. INGRAM
- ◆ b. St. Thomas, Ontario, 1850
- ◆ d. Rossland, B.C., Dec. 1905

When one compares John Ingram to more famous lawmen such as Dodge City's Wyatt Earp and Bat Masterson, and Abilene's "Wild Bill" Hickok what is seen is a man who makes those three worthies appear as mild-mannered gentlemen.

Ingram spent twenty-nine of his forty-four years as an active lawman. During those twenty-nine years he tamed both Winnipeg and Calgary, spent a couple of years in Montana as either a city marshal or a sheriff (the records fail to show his exact capacity) then returned to Canada to tame the rowdy town of Rossland, B.C. Between the time he left Alberta and his reappearance in British Columbia, he is thought to have served as a lawman in Great Falls, Montana, but very little is known of that short period in his life.

Ingram was born in St. Thomas, a small town in the province of Ontario. He spent his boyhood, as did most boys of the era, neither showing a great deal of promise in the scholastic field of endeavor nor showing any ambition to enter the trades. He was of an average family, went to school regularly, attended Sunday School and played in the fields and side streets of the town. When he was sixteen, he obtained employment, toiling at a variety of jobs in a number of shops and on farms that dotted the landscape. By the time he was in his late teens he was thoroughly bored with the tameness of St. Thomas.

So, like many young men, he drifted west with the restless

waves of settlers, hunters, miners and ne'er-do-wells. Arriving in what is now Manitoba in 1870 he worked here and there, trapped a little and herded horses for homesteaders and ranchers now and then. The wilderness life agreed with him while the rigid conditions turned his rawboned body into a powerhouse of strength. Somewhere along the way he learned the rudiments of bare-knuckle boxing.

In the spring of 1873 the twenty-two-year-old drifter arrived in Winnipeg, a wild, near-lawless town with twenty-eight saloons, several brothels and a number of gambling places. He soon established himself as a rough and ready man, one not to be trifled with. His brawls in the Red Saloon, which seems to have been his favorite watering hole, became the stuff of legend although his fights in The Pride of the West Saloon and others were quite spectacular as well.

Manitoba at the time was policed by a territorial police force of a few dozen overworked men. The force, headquartered at Fort Garry, operated under authority from Ottawa but its future was in a state of uncertainty. Ottawa was already forming up the NWMP which, it hoped, could police the entire Northwest Territories within the next year or two. In the meantime the thinly spread territorial force did the best it could to keep the peace.

The following year Ottawa concluded the NWMP would not be large enough to handle the entire Northwest Territory and began recruiting men to augment the territorial force. (The vast area measured 758,000 square miles in its south zone alone. The north zone measured another 1.5 million square miles.) John Ingram, deciding he would make a fine policeman, joined the small force and was assigned a district. He found he enjoyed life as a policeman, did his work quietly and effectively, collected taxes, shot stray dogs, made sure riders kept their horses off the sidewalks, made a few arrests and kept order in the small towns under his control.

The new constable rarely carried a pistol, though he certainly knew how to use one. It was soon clear to all that he preferred to make an arrest by clubbing the suspect into submission with his massive fists. He made his name the day he arrested Ambroise Lepine, a particularly nasty fellow who was wanted on murder charges. Ingram made the arrest through the simple expediency of walking up to Lepine, putting him off guard by greeting him as he would an old friend, then knocking him out with a well-placed left hook to the head. Lepine regained consciousness to find himself locked securely behind bars.

In 1874, Winnipeg was incorporated as a city and as such was entitled to form its own official police force. Ingram was offered the position, accepted, and was duly sworn in as Chief of Police. He immediately set about taming the city.

Ingram's only problem, an ongoing one it turned out, was his love for wine and women, both of which he indulged in lavishly. His downfall began the day Carrie Lyons, an Ontario madam famous in her own right, arrived in the roaring new city with five girls: Ella Lewis, Fannie Ellsworth, Carrie Rowland, Nellie Foster and Addie Booth. Lyons leased a large house where she established her pleasure palace and in so doing became Winnipeg's first madam. Other houses had been established longer but none had been controlled by a madam.

Ingram knew nothing would remove the red-light district, nor did he want to see it go. He was happy just to regulate its inhabitants and keep them separated from those in the "nice" part of town. So long as the gamblers, girls and saloon owners behaved themselves and stayed within the west end of town, he did not interfere with their share of the free enterprise system that flourished in the city. Having established the northern equivalent of Abilene's famed deadline (the boundary separating the "decent" part of town from the red-light district), Ingram made certain the boundaries were respected. The deadline remained inviolate for the duration of his short tenure as police chief.

Carrie Lyons' girls soon had the youthful chief wrapped around their pretty fingers and Ingram began to spend his evenings at Madam Lyons' house. Eventually this reached the ears of the respectable taxpaying public, most of whom felt a police chief—in particular theirs—should show a little more self-discipline. Then two of his constables made a complaint about Ingram's absences from duty during the day. Their complaint stated he was rarely available when they needed him. His supporters retorted that the assertion was nonsense. Everyone knew where Ingram could be found. Certainly the complaining constables should have known where their chief was most of the time.

The city council addressed the matter. Alderman John Villiers, an avowed opponent of the red light district with or without a deadline, publicly denounced Ingram by charging negligence of duty.

He suggested Ingram was maintaining order in the red light district by running a protection racket. Ingram, outraged by the charge, sued Villiers.

Before the case could be heard a surprise raid on Carrie's house one night in June, 1875, by the two constables who had first complained, netted Ingram among the "found-ins." Next morning Ingram, disgraced, appeared before a judge and was fined $8 plus $2 court costs. He was then promptly fired. He had lasted less than a year—but Winnipeg was much tamer than she had ever been in years past.

Ingram remained in Winnipeg working at various jobs, boxing professionally and drinking in the many saloons that dotted the city. His three favorites remained the Red Saloon, The Pride of the West Saloon and the Prairie Saloon. He fought in them all, usually in a ring as a winner-take-all prizefighter but sometimes just for the fun of it. He was arrested for brawling on occasion but always paid his fines and walked away a free man. Eventually he departed Winnipeg and was seen there no more.

Ingram next surfaces as a lawman in Calgary. In 1884 he was hired by the newly incorporated city to take charge of its new police force. His appointment was a calculated risk on the part of the city council. The councilmen were well aware of his reputation in Winnipeg but Calgary needed a no-nonsense lawman with the will to instill law and order and tough enough to convince the resident bad hats to toe the mark. He also had to be able to persuade visiting cowboys to leave their attitudes in their trail camps. Besides, nine years had elapsed—plenty of time for Ingram to have matured.

The risk paid off. Within two months Ingram, still without firing a single shot, had battered the town's felons into submission. Most, such as two identified only as "Crackerbox" Bill and "Bulldog" Kelly, both ruffians and leaders within the criminal community, quietly left town while others stayed but thereafter kept out of trouble.

Ingram and Calgary complemented each other. He was the traditional picture of a marshal of the Old West cow towns. He could be seen strolling the tough streets his badge glinting in the sunlight, hat set flat-a-back at a jaunty angle, mouth set in a hard line or chewing studiously on the stub of a black cigar clenched in his teeth. The only thing missing was a gun strapped to his belt. As in

Winnipeg, he was never seen armed. If he carried a gun, it was well concealed beneath his black frock coat.

Ingram, though respected, was not a well-loved figure. The town's wealthier citizens would have nothing to do with him on a social basis, the city council that paid his ample wage grudgingly tolerated his methods and the toughs and bullies who had long had things their own way kept a respectful distance. He ran his office from the back room of a pool hall. He hired two constables with dispositions similar to his own—Robert Barker, who also held the title of truant officer, and Robert Barton, who also served as license inspector and pound keeper. Never once did he ponder the relative values of both sides of a story—he decided unilaterally which of the combatants was wrong and that person was arrested. In cases where he could not immediately decide, he would arrest both leaving it to the judge to pass final judgement.

He was criticized on occasion for handing a beating to the wrong man but nothing further was ever done. Calgary in 1884 was as rough a cow town as any on either side of the border. It was a town where bartenders routinely assaulted patrons for downing two shots of whiskey then trying to pay for only one. If such a drinker was too tough to fight, the bartender would level his shotgun at him until payment was made or the police arrived. On occasion the trigger was pulled. Calgary was a tough town despite the efforts of some latter day historians who keep insisting the Canadian frontier was not violent. Certainly the violence never equaled that of Abilene, Newton, Ellsworth or Dodge City—and it was certainly not constant—but it was there nonetheless.

John Ingram tamed Calgary as he had Winnipeg by the unflinching use of his rugged fists, his no-nonsense approach and the never denied possibility that, concealed under his coat, there lurked a Colt pistol of large and deadly caliber. Anyone who did not like his methods could select one of two choices—comply with Ingram's rules or get out of town.

Only once did it appear that his disposition might change. That was the year in which he fell in love. In July, 1887, he announced his engagement to an English girl. Calgary wondered, perhaps hopefully, if Ingram was mellowing.

In October, 1887, Ingram married Edith Oake, a pretty woman from a small English town called Hyde. In the hope that married life might soothe his savage breast the citizens of the town's tenderloin buried the hatchets, pooled their resources and, a week before the ceremony, threw him a bachelor party that lasted three days. They were doomed to disappointment. Edith did absolutely nothing to curb his ardor for law and order—his philosophy remained the same: "Do things my way or hit the highway."

In 1887 Ingram's enemies found an ally in the editor of the Calgary *Herald* who began a campaign to rid the city of its tough police chief. In February, 1888, Ingram bowed to the pressure and resigned. His two equally tough constables left with him. He had reigned supreme for four years, a very long time for a lawman in the days of the Old West when most city marshals or police chiefs, on either side of the border, lasted an average of six months.

Ingram's resignation was regretted almost immediately. Within two months the *Herald*'s editor was lamenting that the rollicking town was once again in the hands of the toughs and cutthroats. May Buchanan, a madam of much notoriety, who had been operating her house of joy on a greatly subdued scale rather than run afoul of Ingram, lost no time in rescheduling her hours of business and soon had her house operating the better part of twenty-four hours a day plus Sunday afternoons (the girls were allowed the morning and evening off to attend church). The saloons became raucous once again as the town returned to its former near-lawless chaos.

As if to rub the *Herald*'s editorial nose in the dirt of its own making, Ingram accepted a job managing two hotels, The Palace and The Royal. These became the only establishments in town to enjoy ongoing peace and quiet. Then, in 1890 after his point had been well taken, he and Edith left for Great Falls, Montana, where they lived until 1896 when they moved north once again, this time to Rossland, B.C.

In 1896 Rossland was one of the few towns still roaring in western Canada. The city council asked Ingram if he would be interested in moving in as police chief to rebuild the police force that had more or less collapsed with the departure of Jack Kirkup. (Kirkup, a B.C. Police constable, had tamed Rossland with the same methods used by Ingram but when he left the town quickly reverted to old habits.) Ingram accepted the offer, arrived in town without much fanfare and within six weeks had subdued Rossland by the same tough methods he had used in Winnipeg and Calgary.

Rossland was to know peaceful order from that day forward. The saloons that remained were run in a businesslike manner. The gamblers left town almost in a body and the crime rate dropped to manageable levels. Ingram, it seemed, had also mellowed. He no longer worked, as he had in Calgary, from a tiny room in a pool hall but set up his office in the city hall—and he was accessible and he could be found when he was needed. However, he had never learned political skills, knew nothing of city hall infighting and had troubles dealing with local politicians.

Ingram resigned in 1901 when a political enemy was elected mayor but stayed in town working for a mining company as a security consultant. He returned to the position of police chief in 1902 when the mayor was defeated in his reelection bid. He seemed happy enough in his return to the police force but it was a false happiness. Times had changed too much for the old-style lawman.

Indeed, the Canadian west had changed and Rossland had changed with it. Ingram, however, was unable to change. The town was now too quiet for both his liking and his methods. In 1903, thoroughly bored, he turned in his badge for the final time. John Ingram, the first official police chief appointed in western Canada, had decided he would never return to a policeman's role. Edith was happy—at least until he told her about the job he had accepted.

Ingram had hired on with The Silver Star Mining Ltd., for the dangerous work of what was known as a "dynamite man." The dynamite man's job was to tend the TNT supplies, ensure the sticks were kept at the proper temperature and prepare the fuses to be used the following day. Dynamite men were paid much higher than an average miner but their risk levels were such that insurance agents took great pains to avoid them. It was work Ingram enjoyed for it held the type of danger he had always sought after. This time, however, he was not dealing with an enemy he could intimidate with his massive fists or simply club into submission. Nonetheless, he fitted into the role, learned the meaning of caution and was with the company for almost three years. The three years were happy ones for Edith who had blended nicely into Rossland society and got along well with everyone.

On December 17, 1905, a cold Sunday, Ingram was in the camp's main powder shack preparing fuses for Monday's work. Perhaps he forgot where he was and lit one of his black cigars or maybe the dynamite sticks stored nearby had thawed enough to leak some of their volatile nitroglycerin. No one will ever know. Suddenly a terrific explosion rent the morning air. The shack was blown asunder leaving only a huge hole fifty feet across and ten feet deep plus a strew of shattered lumber to attest to its former existence. Twenty men who were lounging nearby were injured, some seriously; but Ingram was the sole fatality. His shattered body was found 500 feet away. The condition of the body indicated he had been at the very center of the blast. The man whose methods of law enforcement makes those of more famous lawmen pale in comparison was dead at age fifty-five.

On December 20, 1905, his body was put aboard a train and returned to St. Thomas, Ontario, for interment in the family plot. There is no record of Edith's destiny.

CHAPTER 21

The Tragedy of Bad Young Man

BAD YOUNG MAN *a.k.a.* Charcoal
◆ b. 1875
◆ d. March 16, 1897

This is the story of a tragedy involving an unfaithful wife, a cuckolded husband and a misunderstanding of the justice system. It resulted in a murder, an attempted murder, a flight from the law, another murder, a fantastic saga of survival in a blizzard and an unusual hanging.

The story begins in 1875 when Bad Young Man was born into the Blood tribe on the Sarcee Reserve near Calgary. Bad Young Man's birth was hardly noticed and of interest to very few. His father was not a chief nor had he been even a warrior of note; his mother was not the daughter of a chief nor did she possess great beauty or other characteristics that would cause her to stand out from the dozens of other women who toiled for their husbands. When she named her baby Bad Young Man, she was following the ancient custom of naming a child for the first thing seen outdoors following the birth.

In some tribes of that era it was the father who named his sons, in others the mother did the naming. In paternal tribes naming was often done only after a period of time during which the new father communed with the spirits of his family in search of a sign that would be made to him. It was this custom that gave names such as Red Hawk, Sitting Bull and Running Bear. Sons of chiefs were always named in this fashion. (Sitting Bull's original name meant slow moving. When he was in his teens he fought so bravely in an inter-tribal war his father renamed him following a dream in which a bull buffalo approached the young warrior and sat before him in submission. His father realized the dream was an omen and he immediately changed his son's name to Sitting Bull.)

In maternal tribes the new child was named by the mother who drew the name from the first thing she saw. Names such as Wild Horse Standing, Sounding Sky (inspired by thunder rolling) and Gray Cloud were the result of this practice. Perhaps the first thing this particular mother had seen had been the reservation's rogue. No one knows or should even hazard a guess.

Bad Young Man, however, was destined to answer to two names for he soon acquired a nickname that was not particularly flattering. The child was of very dark complexion, not usual among the Plains Indians who were rarely darker than a white man with a healthy tan. By the time he was seven or eight his skin was the hue of the charred wood in the camp's fires. Indian children, no less unfeeling toward their contemporaries than white children, began to call the boy Charcoal. By the time he entered his teen years many had forgotten his real name. To nearly everyone he was simply Charcoal. Nonetheless, this does not appear to have affected his personality or to have embittered him to the society in which he lived.

The whites he dealt with off and on were neither impressed with nor mindful of the young man. He worked occasionally for nearby farmers and ranchers doing field work and hiring out for the annual spring roundup and calf branding. When he worked, he put in a solid day's toil but, as with most of his friends, he had no real liking for steady employment. He spent much of his time in the hills trapping and hunting. He was married to five women at the same time, sired two children and managed to build a reasonable shack to house his large family. He also acquired a small herd of horses along the way. He had no quarrel with the missionaries who enticed his children into school—when they could corral them long enough for lessons—and the NWMP officers who patrolled the area had no reason to concern themselves with him. He never gave trouble to the ranchers or farmers, was never questioned about missing horses and, so far as is known, was never accused by shopkeepers of stealing from their shelves. Not all the inhabitants of the reservation could make that claim.

Charcoal grew to manhood with nothing to distinguish himself in any particular way and remained so for the most part. He was unique only in possessing a complexion that caused him to stand out in a crowd in much the same way as would a pine tree in an alder grove.

Like all young men, Charcoal eventually met a young woman who stole his heart. In fact, over the next couple of years he met four such women, all of whom he married within the traditional laws of the Bloods. The two children he fathered were of one of the wives. Had he remained satisfied with his four original wives, his life would likely have remained uneventful. Unfortunately, Bad Young Man had an insatiable eye for the ladies.

Operating on the theory that if four wives were good then five would be better, he became attracted to a winsome sixteen year old named Pretty Wolverine. Following the traditional courtship customs of his people, he went to the girl's father and asked for her hand in marriage. He offered the patriarch a gift of horses, furs and a good rifle to fortify his claim that he would make a good son-in-law. The gifts were accepted and Pretty Wolverine was given over to Bad Young Man. The wedding, celebrated in late 1895 or early 1896, was well attended as was the ceremonial feast.

Pretty Wolverine unfortunately did not have the same intense feelings for Bad Young Man that he held for her. For a time she played the role of dutiful wife, but the fire of her ardor cooled about the same time as the embers that had roasted the meat for the wedding feast.

About July of 1896 she began to cast flirtatious eyes toward her immediate neighbor, a handsome young brave named Medicine Pipe Stem. The two carried on a torrid affair they thought was discreet but of which everyone was aware except the deceived husband. If Pretty Wolverine thought she could keep her trysts with Medicine Pipe Stem secret from her husband she was badly mistaken. Even the most gullible of cuckolded husbands is bound to find out what is going on sooner or later. Bad Young Man found out about Pretty Wolverine and Medicine Pipe Stem on October 13, 1896.

On that fateful day, a crisp autumn Monday, Bad Young Man, his wives and others of the village were doing field work for a nearby rancher. Also present in the work force was Medicine Pipe Stem. Midway into the morning Bad Young Man saw Pretty Wolverine and Medicine Pipe Stem edging closer to the outer perimeter of the field. He watched as they slipped away into the bushes; he waited a few minutes then proceeded to follow them.

Bad Young Man tracked the pair to an unused root cellar. Looking through a large hole in the siding, he saw his young bride and Medicine Pipe Stem lying on the floor in passionate embrace. After a short personal debate, Bad Young Man retreated from the place, ran the distance to his shack, took his rifle from its resting place and returned to the root cellar. Looking through the hole in the wall he saw the two still on the floor. He leveled the rifle toward the lovers and levered a bullet into the breach.

What happened in the next few minutes was never fully known until November 9, 1946, when Pretty Wolverine, then sixty-six years of age and within an hour of death, related the story to a group of friends and a couple of interested Alberta historians. She had kept the details of Medicine Pipe Stem's killing her secret until that day.

In her narrative Pretty Wolverine told the group that she and Medicine Pipe Stem had gone to root cellar shortly after they had begun the day's work in the field. She had no idea that Bad Young Man knew anything about the affair.

She told how she and her paramour were in an embrace on the dirt floor, quite oblivious to anything, when a sharp noise was heard. Medicine Pipe Stem turned to determine what the noise was and where it was coming from and found himself looking directly into the muzzle of a rifle. What the pair had heard had been the distinctive "click-click" that is made when a bullet is levered into the breach of a repeating rifle. Before he could react, the rifle barked once. Medicine Pipe Stem, a small bullet hole directly between his eyes and a large one at the back of his head, fell back across the terrified girl.

Pretty Wolverine said she could see her husband standing, rifle in hand, looking down at her. Fully expecting the rifle to speak once again she closed her eyes to await the impact of a bullet striking her breast. For what seemed an eternity she lay in terror—but there was no further sound. She remained under the body of the dead man for some time before mustering enough courage to open her eyes. Bad Young Man was nowhere to be seen. He had, inexplicitly, spared his unfaithful wife.

Pretty Wolverine pushed against the dead weight of her erstwhile lover's body, rolled out from under him, gathered her clothing and fled from the cellar to a bush near the shack. To her relief she saw the shack was empty, so she went inside and remained there all day weeping while cowering in a corner. That night she slipped out and ran to her father's home. Whether she told him her story is not known but if she did he kept it to himself.

The following morning the entire area knew that Medicine Pipe Stem was dead, coldly murdered, and that Bad Young Man was on the run. Pretty Wolverine never saw her husband again and said nothing of that morning until she spoke of it on her death bed.

The shack was empty when Pretty Wolverine returned to it because Bad Young Man, fully aware that he would be hunted as a killer, had decided to run. He took his four wives and the two children and headed for the bush country. Then he did a very foolish thing. The following day he left his family in the bush to return to the reservation. There he announced to a gathering of his neighbors that he was not going to be taken alive for the killing of Medicine Pipe Stem. The astounded listeners then heard him declare he intended to end his days in a blaze of terror.

"I will not hang for the death of Medicine Pipe Stem," he told them.

"Turn yourself in," he was told. "You are the aggrieved husband."

"I am an Indian who has killed another," he replied, "and there is no justice for such a man under the white man's law."

"I will not hang," he repeated. "I will be killed rather than surrender. I will settle some scores. First, I will kill Wilson, then I will kill Red Crow."

Why he intended to kill Red Crow, the reservation's chief he gave no reason. Neither did he explain his reason for wanting to kill James Wilson, who was the Indian Agent. The statement about Wilson did not cause any furor among the crowd but the threat against Red Crow was a serious mistake. Red Crow was much loved by his people and they did not take kindly to threats against the respected chief. When Bad Young Man made that threat he effectively turned his people against him. Even his own family disowned the west's newest renegade. (Red Crow spent the next few weeks in his house carefully avoiding windows. His people also kept watch. The elderly chief emerged only after his guardians deemed it safe.)

At that point Bad Young Man rode away with a wild whoop, the cry of the brave on his way to battle. Later that evening he returned unseen to the reservation. Determining that Wilson's house was occupied, he hid in the shadows some distance away and waited until he saw Wilson standing at a window. Raising his rifle, he fired one shot.

The distance was not very great but the darkness made sighting difficult. Although his bullet found the mark and Wilson fell, the bullet had not hit any vital organ. Wilson was only wounded and recovered quickly.

By shooting James Wilson, Bad Young Man had crossed the line. It was bad enough that he killed Medicine Pipe Stem but considering the circumstances had he turned himself in without further ado he would likely have been sentenced only to a jail term. Juries in 1896 took lenient views toward husbands who killed men who stole wives. The history of the Old West shows no discernable differences in verdicts rendered by juries in such trials. The law was actually very equitable to both Indian and white husbands in these cases; and to that point Bad Young Man had harmed no one else. The jail term would have been more for the attempt against James Wilson's well being than for the killing of Medicine Pipe Stem.

But Bad Young Man did not understand the law as it applied to such cases. He had seen Indians pronounced guilty while seeing white men, charged with similar offenses, freed. He saw no reason why he would not become one of the former. As a result he chose to become a fugitive.

With his women and children in tow, Bad Young Man went deeper into the bush. He was spotted a few days later by a police patrol and fired on the officers. Following a short gun battle the patrol moved in only to discover that Bad Young Man had escaped with two wives and one child. The remaining women and the child were returned to the reservation.

Bolstered by reinforcements the patrol returned to the trail. For four weeks they tracked the small party with no success. During that time the fugitive one night snuck into the town of Cardston, probably intending to steal food. He was seen and chased. In his flight he took a shot at an NWMP corporal who ducked for cover and in so doing lost sight of the fleeing man.

On November 11 a patrol caught up with Bad Young Man again, this time near Pinscher Creek. The officer in charge, Sgt. W. B. Wilde, holding a white cloth in one hand and placing his rifle across the saddle pommel in the traditional sign of asking for a peace parley, rode slowly toward the man. Had Bad Young Man spoken with the officer he might have realized that he was not likely to hang for murder. Instead, he shot Wilde out of the saddle. Wilde died a few minutes later. Bad Young Man fled, leaving his remaining wives and child in the bush. At least they were safe now, probably overjoyed when told they would be returned to the reservation. Bad Young Man, however, was gone again.

The corporal who became patrol leader on Wilde's death looked at the sky and knew at once the weather was about to take a bad turn. He ordered his men to bundle the women and child into the warmest clothing available and to double up on the horses (ride two on a horse). They were fairly close to Fort MacLeod but should the impending storm hit sooner than he could forecast they would all be serious trouble. He gave the signal to head out and the patrol broke into a rapid pace. They arrived at their destination as the snow began to swirl around them. They had been fortunate to have had the increasing wind at their backs.

By midnight conditions had become truly bad. This was a prairie storm of great severity in a land known for severe blizzards. First the wind began to sweep down from the north. The howling Arctic wind, gusting in excess of sixty miles per hour, drove the snow, the likes of which had not been seen in years. Trees snapped and branches crashed to earth. Trails and wagon roads were covered within hours by drifting snow that obliterated all sign of wheel ruts. Overnight the snow reached depths of three feet and when dawn broke over the land visibility was less than fifty feet. The entire prairie had become a vast white field bereft of visible trails or roads. For three days the blizzard raged unabated.

The storm raged and when it finally ceased the temperature dropped even further until it was at the coldest levels in years. Many felt the fugitive would have surely perished for he had no food and was not adequately dressed. His odds for survival were poor indeed.

But Bad Young Man, in defiance of all the odds, managed to survive the worst winter conditions imaginable; and he did so without stopping to build shelter or light a fire or eat. Throughout the entire storm and after it had stopped he had struggled northward through drifts of waist-deep snow while facing directly into the teeth of that overpowering Arctic wind. How he managed such a feat remains to this day one of the west's greatest examples of human endurance. Somehow he was able to travel more than seventy miles until he came to the shack occupied by two of his brothers, Bear's Backbone and Left Hand. His trek had taken almost three weeks.

Bad Young Man arrived at the shack during a cold December night. He was gaunt, starving and approaching delirium from the effects of the cold. His feet and hands were frozen. His ears were so badly frozen, they were as bluish white as a cube of ice. Had anyone even touched his ears they would likely have broken from his head.

At first the brothers did not recognize the strange apparition who scratched feebly at their door but they took him in, wrapped him in blankets and spooned venison broth into him. After three days he slowly regained his senses. As his ears and hands thawed, his cries of agony were heart rendering for nothing is more painful than the return of blood to frozen limbs and appendages.

By this point Bad Young Man was likely on the verge of the madness that would turn his brothers against him. As the days passed, Bad Young Man gained in strength but his frozen feet would not respond to either warmth or herbal balms. He was never to regain the use of his legs. He needed medical help that his brothers could not offer but he refused to allow them to seek such help. For several more days they kept him as comfortable as they could even as his madness increased.

Knowing his brothers intended to remove him to a hospital in nearby Calgary he somehow got hold of a pistol. He virtually held the pair prisoners, abusing them and threatening to shoot them if they so much as suggested he be turned in. He held the upper hand for several days by refusing to allow them to leave the shack or even to get too close to the door in case one might attempt to break free. The pistol was never out of his hand. His mad eyes followed their every move. At any moment he might kill them both—and they knew it.

Finally the frightened brothers saw a way to escape his excesses and threats. They devised some trick that saw him relax his vigil and then managed to wrest the gun from his grip. They tied him to his chair and Left Hand rode to Calgary where he informed the police that the manhunt was over. Bad Young Man, he who was better known to all as Charcoal, was taken into custody and transported to the hospital in Calgary.

There he recovered somewhat but was a sorry shell of his former robust physique. Still, he was well enough to be taken to the jail at Fort MacLeod where he would stand trial for the murder of Sgt. Wilde.

His trial got underway in January, 1897. He was found guilty and sentenced to hang. The trial judge set the date for March 16 to allow time for the mandatory appeal. The appeal was denied and on that date, at 7:00 a.m., the prisoner was tied securely to a wooden chair, removed from his cell and carried to the scaffold up the steps and placed on the trap door. There, still seated, the hood was placed over his head and the rope was looped around his neck. The guards stepped back, the hangman pulled a lever and the trap door swung open.

Lest anyone get the impression that being carried on a chair to the gallows implies Bad Young Man did not meet his death with courage (although he did attempt suicide while awaiting the date), the reason for this action should be explained. During his two months in jail awaiting his date with the hangman he lost the ability to walk for he could no longer use his legs, a consequence of the December storm ordeal. The decision was made that he should be secured to a sturdy wooden chair and conveyed in this manner to the scaffold. When the lever was pulled, Bad Young Man and his chair plunged downward.

Bad Young Man was about twenty-seven years old the day he died.

The direct cause for Bad Young Man's woes, Pretty Wolverine, wasted no time in lamenting his hanging. She quickly married again, and again, and again until she eventually compiled a list of five husbands. She remained on the reservation but her life was not at all spectacular. She lived in self-imposed isolation with whatever man she was married to at the time and generally minded her own affairs in a quiet way. Once in awhile some writer or reporter would seek her out to ask her version of what had happened to drive Bad Young Man to violence but she would never discuss the subject. On the occasions when the visitors became insistent she would turn violent ordering the inquisitive ones away from her property. Sometimes she backed her words with a rifle. Even the most persistent reporters quickly fled when Pretty Wolverine pointed a rifle their way.

She remained close lipped until the day of her death when she finally related her part in the tragedy.

Also by E.C. (TED) MEYERS

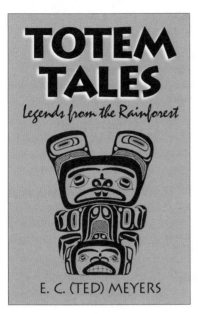

Totem Tales
**Legends from
the Rainforest**
E. C. (Ted) Meyers
ISBN 0-88839-468-3
5.5 x 8.5, sc
80 pages

Basic Bush Survival
E. C. (Ted) Meyers
ISBN 0-88839-399-7
5.5 x 8.5, sc
160 pages